ENDORSEMENTS

"This guidepost will be of great benefit to anyone or organization desiring to create a culture of others-focused service. We own a secular business that is very much a ministry to us. Upon reading the initial draft of *God's Work—God's Way*, we knew this would become part of our business doctrine. The document so clearly identifies and communicates how the Lord we serve expects us to conduct our daily business. The book provides us with illustrations of how to walk this out and what that may look like on a practical level. Every Tuesday morning, we spend time with our staff in devotion, sharing, and prayer for one another. This book and the principles it supports have become part of that time. You can see the changes in attitudes when people really understand God's leading in very practical terms for their walk in all areas of life.

In these pages you will see how God orchestrates the development of a ministry and its people. The principles established are all scripturally based and supported. Marcia Mitchell, founder and CEO of the Little Light House for the first forty years of its history, illustrates how the Lord walked the Little Light House family through trials, failure, blessing, and success in a faithful, loving manner. Some of the stories will make you cry while others will build your faith and confidence in the mighty God we serve. The book as a whole will inspire you to rethink every aspect of your business as you seek to determine if you are carrying out your work and your life, God's way."

- Kim and Scott Burnett
Owners, Burnett Inc. Windows and Siding

"The persistence and faith illustrated in Marcia's book is more than just a collection of words, but an accurate and poignant picture of the life Marcia has led. The legacy of her ministry is evident, not as something she has accomplished alone, but as something God has accomplished through her and the many who have been inspired by her vision. With stories of honest struggles and bold victories, this book challenges every reader to take on the improbable and trust God with the impossible. I've been proud to call Marcia my friend for the past thirty years, and I'm thankful to see her story told in such a refreshing, hopeful way."

- Larry Thompson
Pastor Emeritus, First Baptist Church of Fort Lauderdale

"After pastoring for over forty years, it was both refreshing and challenging to read *God's Work—God's Way*. I had the privilege of watching these principles lived out at the Little Light House before they were ever documented. Marcia has given us a valuable, practical, and Biblical approach to all who believe that the means must be as Godly as the ends."
- *Pastor Paul Taylor*
Anthem Church, Tulsa, Oklahoma

"For years I have looked for a book that detailed scriptural principles to help me run my business. This book sets a golden standard to measure sound decisions by."
- *Denise Wright*
Wright Home Team Realtors

"Is God that big? That good? That loving? In her new book, Marcia Mitchell shares that He indeed is! I was also encouraged as I witnessed through my reading the truth that when Biblical foundational principles are applied without compromise, God shows up, He is glorified, and lives are touched and changed! *God's Work—God's Way* is not just the title of this book but also how ministry should be."
- *Tou Chang*
Bonder for NORDAM

"God's Word is never failing. Marcia Mitchell has shared her firsthand experiences from over the past four decades of how to use Biblical principles to see God's hand move in everyday situations. Anyone who is in ministry, owns a business, and especially individuals who want to experience God in their everyday lives, need to read *God's Work—God's Way*. As you read, I believe you will be greatly impacted by the stories that are shared and know that you can experience God's faithfulness daily in your own personal life."
- *Jean Winfrey*
Executive Director, Little Light House

"John 17:16 NASB says, '*They are not of the world, even as I am not of the world.*'
The Biblical principles found in *God's Work—God's Way* tell us all how to live and work in God's culture, which transcends all other cultures, all generations, and all times. These principles were taught by God through our Lord Jesus Christ and recorded for all time in the Holy Bible. *God's*

Work—God's Way is what we need to help us recognize these principles and be encouraged to live by them as we follow Jesus, our Lord and Savior."

- Linda Steed
Director of Global Impact, Little Light House

"Reading *God's Work—God's Way* gave me a deeper trust in Jesus and renewed my faith that nothing is impossible with God."

- Ellen Stamps
Author, My Years with Corrie

"*God's Work—God's Way* records faithfully observed results in divine blessing. As I read this inspiring book, I was motivated and encouraged by the Biblical truths practiced and shared. I am confident others will experience equal effects."

- Jim Wallis
Pastor Emeritus, Apostolic Faith Congregation, Laverne, OK

"We are all created in God's image—if His principles and precepts are applied in our daily walk, we have the assurance of being successful. *God's Work—God's Way* is an anointed tool which can be applied in both secular and Christian settings. We witnessed firsthand that these Biblical principles really work. From the leadership all the way through the staff and the volunteers, God supernaturally provided inspiration needed for lesson plans, curriculum, as well as physical needs. Thank you, Marcia, for putting into writing what you learned as the Founder and Director of the Little Light House. Many will be blessed as they follow your lead."

- Donald G. Shamblin, PhD, Educator and Marlis Shamblin
Cofounders of Servants Ministry Int'l

"In *Milestones & Miracles*, Marcia Mitchell brought us the moving and inspiring story of her journey to build a future and a hope for children with special needs. In this new book, she lets us in on the Biblical principles behind her extraordinary success. It is essential reading for anyone who wants to know how to make their God-inspired dream a reality!"

- Dr. Colin Harbinson
International Director, StoneWorks Global Arts Initiative

GOD'S WORK
GOD'S WAY

A MUST-READ FOR THOSE WHO ARE CALLED TO
TAKE ON THE IMPROBABLE AND TRUST GOD
WITH THE IMPOSSIBLE

MARCIA MITCHELL

DEDICATION

This book is dedicated to the Little Light House Board of Directors who have been uncompromisingly committed to doing God's work, God's way. I will be forever grateful to you for recognizing the importance of recording these principles for future generations.

TABLE OF CONTENTS

ACKNOWLEDGMENTS

I want to thank Kim and Scott Burnett for the foresight they demonstrated in asking me to document the Little Light House foundational Biblical principles for the Little Light House. It was their encouragement to do so, which prompted me to write *God's Work—God's Way* as a historical reflection of how God imparted those key principles to us and etched the truth of them on our hearts.

I also want to acknowledge Denise Wright, Paul Taylor, and Jean Winfrey for believing in the need for this book and serving as my Barnabas and constant source of encouragement to write it.

My biggest and perhaps most heartfelt thanks go out to my dear friend and gifted coworker Susie Scarpitti who served as my editor for this project. Susie, your brilliance in editing is only exceeded by your amazing ability to encourage and affirm and your sensitivity to do so when I most needed it. Your skills are amazing and your precious spirit made working with you pure joy. This book would not have been possible without you and I will be forever grateful to you for helping me birth it. You are one in a million!

To the Staff of the Little Light House: Your beautiful hearts are reflected on the pages of this book, but there are no words which adequately capture the level of dedication and devotion to God's special children and to the Almighty which I see in you. Thank you for your ongoing commitment to doing God's work, God's way.

A special thank you to pastor Paul Taylor, Maureen and Colin Harbinson, Marlis and Donald Shamblin, Marj Miller, Ellen Stamps, Pastor James Wallis, Pastor Larry Thompson, Jean Winfrey, Denise Wright, Tou Chang, Linda Steed, Phil Mitchell, and Missy Mitchell for your untiring willingness to review the manuscript of this book from a Biblical, historical, and readability perspective. I treasured your input and will always be grateful for the time you dedicated to this project and your loving support of it.

To Phil Mitchell and Missy Mitchell, my loving husband and daughter, thank you for your patience and encouragement over the four years it took me to complete this book. I love you to the moon and back and will be forever grateful for your understanding and support.

And finally, to my Heavenly Father, who authored these marvelous principles and who served as my constant companion, encouragement, comfort, and guide as I attempted to share them with my world.

FOREWORD

I've witnessed it with my own eyes, and I'll call it what it is—a twenty-first-century miracle. A twenty-first-century miracle called the Little Light House, and its very existence, not to mention the impact it is having across the globe, raises gripping questions which beg for logical explanations.

How could a tiny, unknown, fledgling ministry which started out with only a dream and a prayer become a destination for thousands of college and career students as well as individuals and groups from all across the globe?

How could a center with its simple beginnings conceivably offer the most technologically advanced educational and therapeutic training methods available anywhere in the nation and possibly the world?

How could a private school for children with special needs provide the highest standard of educational and therapeutic services without the benefit of insurance reimbursements or any type of government or United Way funding?

How could such a school remain debt-free for more than four decades and even build a $16,500,000 state-of-the-art facility and move in debt-free?

How is it that so many children whom doctors have said would never walk and never talk enter the Little Light House "unable" and leave the Little Light House "able" to do those very things and more?

Frankly, the human mind can't help but wonder, how does all of this happen?

The short answer to all of these questions could be summed up by a quote which has hung in the office of the Little Light House founder, Marcia Mitchell, since the very early years of the ministry. "God's Work Done God's Way Will Not Lack God's Provision." This strong conviction embraced by Marcia and the Little Light House leadership over the decades has resulted in a ministry which is genuinely committed to operating by Biblical principles and dedicated to bringing glory to God through every aspect of its work. The simple fact is, the Little Light House is what it is today because of the grace and power of God and because Biblical principles are as effective today as the day they were written. The Little Light House is a living testimony that the principles set forth in His Word simply work!

As the Little Light House approached its fortieth anniversary in 2011, Marcia was preparing to retire. Prompted by an appeal from the Board of Directors, she felt compelled to write *God's Work— God's Way* to ensure the scriptural lessons learned over the first forty years of Little Light House history would be remembered and lived out for generations to come.

As you read the standards set forth in *God's Work—God's Way*, you will see they are simple, but not easy to walk out. They often fly in the face of conventional wisdom. But God's ways are not man's ways, and the Little Light House has always been committed to the conviction we must choose whom we will serve and never look back! The far-reaching impact of the Little Light House today is the result of the power, love, and grace of God and an uncompromising commitment to do His work, His way.

Within these pages, I found inspiration, understanding, and hope. I believe you will as well. For that I am deeply grateful to God and to Marcia.

In His Grip,
Kimberly Burnett

BUILDING ON SOLID ROCK

Unless the LORD builds the house, its builders
labor uselessly. Unless the LORD guards the city,
its security forces keep watch uselessly.

– (Psalm 127:1 ISV) –

It was in the fall of 2012 when I began discussing my retirement plans with the Board of Directors of the Little Light House. I was sixty-eight years of age. More than four decades had passed since God had led a friend and me to establish the Christian developmental center for children with special needs.

As I entered into this discussion with the board, I couldn't help but reflect. It didn't seem possible so many years had passed since God first planted the dream of the Little Light House in my heart. Though I remained passionate about the vision God had given me for this ministry, I felt with increased certainty, as surely as God had led me into this calling, He was now leading me in a new direction. To follow His leading meant retiring from my position as CEO of the ministry. I wasn't certain where God was taking me, but I did know He had placed a strong desire in my heart to devote the autumn years of my life to my family and to whatever else He called me to do.

So we began thinking and planning for the transition that would be involved in my retirement. Jean, a gifted coworker who had been by my side for more than thirty-five years, was the perfect one to take on the leadership of the ministry. She had served in a number of capacities over the years and, when not on staff, she had demonstrated her loyalty and devotion to the ministry as a volunteer and board member. Her love and commitment to the Little Light House had never wavered, and she was passionate about the Little Light House ministry and vision.

Over the four previous years, Jean had been responsible for overseeing the day-to-day operation of the center. This had allowed me to begin focusing my attention and time on Little Light House global programs, the Little Light House affiliate, and other new initiative programs for our center. When the time came for me to retire, Jean was God's obvious choice for me to pass the proverbial baton to without question. For certain she would keep Christ as the cornerstone of the Little Light House and see to it that the ministry would continue to operate by the Biblical principles which had become such an integral part of our DNA.

Still, there was concern on the part of the Board of Directors. How could we be assured that, beyond the season of my immediate successor, the Little Light House would remain Christ-centered, dedicated to bringing glory to our Lord God Almighty?

It is widely known that most of the colleges across the United States were established as Bible-proclaiming schools. Yale, Harvard, and even Princeton had rich Christian histories. Yet today these same universities, and countless others across our great nation, bear no resemblance to Christian universities nor offer any hint at ever having had any Biblical foundation. According to Bodie Hodge in a 2007 article in *Answers*, "Accepting a naturalistic worldview and compromising Scripture were the first cracks in the universities' Christian foundations. These cracks led to the collapse of their Christian heritage."[1]

So the question troubling our board was how to ensure the Little Light House commitment to Biblical principles would remain steadfast for generations to come. Every effort had been made over the past four decades to build the Little Light House on the solid rock of God's Word, His power, and His principles. Yet the question remained: what steps could be taken now to make

How could we be assured that the Little Light House would maintain being Christ-centered for generations to come?

certain the ministry would remain Christ-centered and maintain a strong witness for Christ in the future?

With this concern in mind, it was the suggestion of one tenured board member that I create a document outlining the foundational Biblical principles reflected in the core values we had embraced and practiced since the founding of the Little Light House. It was further proposed that, once complete, the documentation be incorporated into the articles and bylaws of the corporation. It was the hope of all concerned that this measure would help to ensure a steadfast commitment to the original Christian values and mission by those who would follow in our footsteps.

It was this same request which prompted the writing of *God's Work—God's Way*. On these pages you will read historical insights as to how God imparted Biblical principles to us, the lessons we gleaned and reasons we now hold these principles to be vital to the future of the Little Light House. After all, it is the commitment to these principles that is the very heartbeat of the Little Light House ministry.

And so it was, that my initial motivation for writing this book was for the benefit of the Little Light House. However, it

1.Bodie Hodge, "Harvard, Yale, Princeton, Oxford—Once Christian?" *Answers Magazine*, June 27, 2007.

is my hope and prayer that other ministries (especially fledgling ministries), Christian business owners, ministry leaders, and totally devoted followers of Christ will benefit from this writing as well. I pray as you look within these pages you will discover the truth and amazing blessing of doing God's work—God's way.

When the foundations are destroyed, what can the righteous do?

– (Psalm 11:3 ISV) –

Therefore whoever hears these sayings of Mine, and does them, I will liken him to a wise man who built his house on the rock: and the rain descended, the floods came, and the winds blew and beat on that house; and it did not fall, for it was founded on the rock. But everyone who hears these sayings of Mine, and does not do them, will be like a foolish man who built his house on the sand: and the rain descended, the floods came, and the winds blew and beat on that house; and it fell. And great was its fall."

– (Matthew 7:24-27 NKJV) –

CHAPTER ONE

LEAP OF FAITH

For we walk by faith, not by sight.

– (2 Corinthians 5:7 NKJV) –

I had been a Christian since the age of twelve. I recall clearly feeling a strong prompting from the Holy Spirit to walk down that long aisle of First Baptist Church in Tulsa, Oklahoma, and profess Jesus Christ as my Lord and Savior. A short while later, I was baptized and I recall the pastor's words: "buried with Him in baptism, raised to walk in newness of life." It was a meaningful moment for me and I remember genuinely desiring to draw near to the heart of God and follow Him all the days of my my life.

From that time on and throughout my teen years and even into college, I was committed to nightly devotionals and Bible reading. I even led a devotional time in my dorm. I leaned on the Lord and spent hours in our little college chapel crying out to Him. I treasured my personal relationship with Christ and relied on Him for everything, from help on my dreaded Geology tests to resisting worldly temptations every college student faces. He was always there for me. He carried me through life's valleys and comforted me when I was down. Through those years, I drew even closer to Him and felt I had an ideal relationship with my Lord. I believed in His love and power with all my heart.

After graduating from college, I was reunited with a lifelong friend. We fell in love, were married, and three years later we were expecting our first child. We were both elated and looked forward to becoming parents. When that day finally arrived, I gave birth to a six-pound, seven-ounce beautiful baby girl. Everything seemed perfect in every way. We had the baby girl I had secretly yearned for all along. We were both ecstatic.

Nothing could have prepared me for the news our pediatrician delivered to us the next morning. Our precious baby girl had been born with a condition which resulted in a visual impairment. We were told her vision would range somewhere between less than normal and blind.

My husband actually handled the news better than I did. I was left crushed and bewildered, asking the question "why" over and over. I felt I had loved the Lord and put Him first in my life since a young teen. I didn't understand why He had allowed this to happen. By God's mercy and grace, over the next few days, I began to realize the "why" didn't really matter. What did matter was the "how." How God could use this situation for good.

The doctors told us to take our baby home and treat her like a normal child. We did so, to the best of our ability. But I knew she had needs beyond what we could meet. As an educator, I was well aware of the critical importance of early intervention. A bit more research confirmed our baby definitely needed such a program. Without it, we would likely see her lag further and further behind developmentally.

So for the next year and a half we searched the Tulsa area for early intervention programs for children with visual impairments. To our utter amazement, there were absolutely no services available for children with visual limitations until the age of six. I knew that was too late. As my research had revealed, many children were often placed in classes for the mentally challenged at the age of six, even though they were simply blind or visually limited. Because they lacked early intervention, they had fallen further and further behind, resulting in significant developmental delays. Knowing this, I knew we had to find a program for her as soon as possible.

Weeks later, we learned about a program in Oklahoma City. We wrote immediately requesting an appointment. Shortly after, we were scheduled for a visit, at which time they evaluated

It is in tackling the seemingly impossible tasks, we learn to completely depend on God.

our daughter and agreed to see her on a monthly basis. They committed to making recommendations following each visit regarding how we could help her progress.

It was only a few months later that, quite by miracle, we met another couple with a child with special needs. Soon, they too had enrolled their child in the monthly program. But it was on one of our joint visits we learned that the type of long-distance program offered to us wouldn't be adequate for a child with such complex needs as their little girl had. "Are you sure there are no services in Tulsa?" the professionals asked. We were certain. We had done extensive research and the results were clear.

It was on the way home we first began to dream about how wonderful it would be to have such a program right where we lived. We decided surely one of the centers, schools, or hospitals in Tulsa would be willing to establish one.

Soon after, we began our search, but it was to no avail. Doctors, directors, and administrators told us over and again, "We're sorry. We just don't have the staff." From others, we heard about their lack of space, or finances. Different reasons but always the same bottom line. They couldn't help us!

Weeks later, one well-meaning pediatrician, hearing of our plight, looked us both in the eye and said the most incredible thing to us. He peered over his reading glasses, sat back in his big office chair, and said quite calmly, "Ladies, if you want this center, you'll have to build it yourselves."

I was incredulous! Furthermore, I was at the end of my rope. Not one professional we had seen had offered to help. And now this? That doctor had to know we didn't have the funds or the resources to start a center for children with special needs, and we certainly didn't have the know-how to begin such a program. I expressed my irritation all the way to the car. We had been sitting in the car for quite some time and I was still expressing my irritation when it suddenly dawned on me that my friend, the mother of the other child, hadn't spoken a word. Instead, she was sitting quietly with the most angelic expression on her face.

"Sheryl, surely you aren't thinking what I think you're thinking." She only smiled. "Sheryl," I exclaimed, "we wouldn't know the first thing about how to start a program like that!" To which she responded with three words: "But God does." Of course I knew that. "But," I continued on, "if those doctors think it would be so expensive (which so many had expressed), I don't even want to think about what it would cost, and we don't have a dime to begin such a program!" Sheryl simply smiled sweetly again and calmly and quietly whispered, "But God does."

I sat speechless for a while as I turned that over and over in my mind. As I did so, I suddenly realized that for the first time in my life I had come face-to-face with a question. Did I really believe what I had always said I believed? Did I really believe in the love and power of God? Did I really believe in a God who could move mountains? For years I had been a Christian and I had professed God could do anything. But suddenly I was confronted with the question: did I really believe it? Could God even establish a center to meet the needs of our little girls and other children like them, when all He had to work with was us?

We were both in our mid-twenties. I was a former speech and drama teacher; Sheryl, a homemaker. Neither of us had even a beginning knowledge (much less experience or formal training) in management, administration, or special education, not to speak of how to establish a non-profit. We had no resources that we knew of, and not an inkling of an idea where or how to even begin.

I was quiet as we headed home. My heart and mind raced as that one question echoed repeatedly in my head. Again, I reflected, "Did I really believe what I had always said I believed?" Did I believe God could do anything, including such an impossible task as the one that loomed ahead of us? It would require a giant leap of faith. I didn't know if I had that kind of faith! Hours later, however, I made up my mind. I had to take that leap of faith or I would never know the answer to my question.

I'm sure our husbands thought we were delusional, but they reluctantly allowed us to move forward. So in the spring of 1972, we dared to believe God for a twentieth-century miracle and took that giant leap of faith. The rest is history.

I believe that kind of leap of faith is involved in any God-sized task. After all, it is in tasks that seem impossible for us, we learn to completely depend on Him.

Ann Kiemel wrote a book called *I Love the Word Impossible*.[2] Ann's whole premise for the book is that you can't have a miracle until you have an impossible situation. God was revealing to me personally this very profound truth.

So whether you are facing a financial challenge, a crisis in business, or the need for resources to establish a ministry, if you know God is leading, take the leap. Believe! We did and in so doing, I received the answer to my question. He really can do anything. We witnessed it firsthand. The next chapters of Little Light House history are living proof.

> *Amen, I say to you, if you have faith the size of a mustard seed, you will say to this mountain, 'Move from here to there,' and it will move. Nothing will be impossible for you.*
>
> — (Matthew 17:20 NABRE) —

---

2. Ann Kiemel Anderson, *I Love the Word Impossible* (Wheaton, IL: Tyndale House, 1976).

CHAPTER TWO

WHAT'S IN YOUR HAND

But Moses said, "They won't believe me! They won't do what I tell them to. They'll say, 'Jehovah never appeared to you!'" "What do you have there in your hand?" the Lord asked him. And he replied, "A shepherd's rod." "Throw it down on the ground," the Lord told him. So he threw it down— and it became a serpent, and Moses ran from it! Then the Lord told him, "Grab it by the tail!" He did, and it became a rod in his hand again! "Do that and they will believe you!" the Lord told him.

– (Exodus 4:1–5 TLB) –

From the moment God placed the dream in our hearts to establish a center for our little girls, and we took that giant leap of faith, there was the ever-pervading concern about how we were going to accomplish the task before us. We lacked funding, contacts, resources, knowledge, and experience. We had no idea how to secure a facility, hire the necessary staff, or recruit the needed volunteers, much less how to pay for the essential supplies and equipment. Neither the cofounder nor I had been married for more than five years and neither possessed substantial savings we could possibly use.

We had no idea how or where to even begin to build a developmental center for children with special needs. We only knew God had spoken to our hearts about starting this center and we felt sure there had to be many more children in need of such services beyond our own. I can remember feeling much like Moses when he found himself staring at the burning bush. I identified with his feelings of inadequacy and the questions he shouted at God. There were moments I wanted to shout the same kind of questions!

Like He did with Moses, God was asking me to lay down my proverbial staff.

Looking back on it years later, it is now easy to see that God dealt with me in much the same way He dealt with Moses. He caused me to look at what was "in my hand." I remember the experience well.

It was about a month after we first sensed God was leading us to start the center. I was out running some errands and as I was driving, I began reflecting on what had taken place in that short amount of time.

Within weeks of hearing the pediatrician tell us that we'd just have to "start the center ourselves," quite by God's orchestration, a little group of ladies had offered to help us conduct a small garage sale. They were dear and they put a great deal of effort into the project, but it rained most of the weekend and less than $100 had been raised. Though appreciative, I knew such a small amount was hardly enough to make any impact on our endeavor. My mind had been consumed with worry and finally, while running those errands, I began to pour my heart out in prayer.

"God, we've been told it will take $2,000–$3,000 just to get the doors of our little school open. Lord, we don't have that kind of money and I don't have a clue where we can get it. I haven't seen that kind of money raised since . . ." Suddenly, my heart skipped a beat. My prayer continued . . ."since the Junior High School musical I directed before I retired!" In that moment, I could sense God smiling and that's when it came to me. Perhaps my drama background could be used to raise the necessary funds to get our doors open. That was all I had. It was the only means I knew to raise funds. Looking back now, I can see, figuratively speaking, THAT'S what was in my hand. That was my shepherd's rod. I knew my drama experience alone couldn't possibly make a difference. But with God's help, I felt it might just work. Like Moses who had been told to throw his staff down, I had to trust God and lay down my proverbial staff or, in this case, my degree in drama and what ability I had to direct a musical, and trust God's power to work through what was in my hand.

I decided to share the idea with the cofounder, and she responded with overwhelming enthusiasm. She encouraged me to call the students who had performed the musical two years before and ask if they'd be willing to give up their summer and repeat the experience to help raise funds to get the doors open for our dream center. That's when fear set in! You know, probably much like Moses experienced when he had to pick the snake up by the tail? I was partly afraid my former students would say yes, and at the same time, I was also afraid they'd say no. If they agreed to it, I knew God would be taking our dream to the next level. While that would be exciting, it was also terrifying to me, for then, there'd be no turning back. Then again, if they said no, I knew we'd be right back where we started with no funding and no means of raising it.

With some fear and trepidation, I began to make the calls. I hadn't seen the students who had made up my musical cast in the two years since we had put on the production. I knew they likely had their summers planned. My mind was spinning. Where could we produce the musical and who would sell tickets? Where would we get the funds to build a set and make new costumes? I couldn't possibly do everything. I'd have to have an enormous amount of help and I had no idea where that help would come from.

But, just as God began demonstrating His ability to work through that shepherd's staff to Moses, God began to dramatically demonstrate His power as soon as I laid down my proverbial staff and began to make those calls.

From that point on, we saw His miracle-working power on a daily basis. The group of women who had put on the garage sale agreed to handle ticket sales and promotions. The male counterpart of their organization provided the funds to produce the play. A center for physically challenged individuals offered to provide their stage and auditorium for us, and some talented friends and volunteers stepped up to build the set, make costumes, and handle the lighting.

Three months later, the musical had been produced and had profited $2,700. Following the last curtain call, God continued to part the waters, providing a small rent-free facility, a dedicated teacher, equipment, supplies, volunteers, and a community who began to embrace our dream.

This scenario would play itself out countless times over the next four decades. Time and again God would remind us to look at what we already had in our hand. As with Moses, it always required a step of faith and a strong trust in God's ability to use an ordinary gift, resource, or talent. But to the day of this writing, God continues to pour out His power when we simply trust, lay down what is in our hand, and obey. Readers, I encourage you, if you are facing a dilemma, and you have a need, seek the Lord. Perhaps He is asking you, "What's in your hand?" When you discover what He has already given you, lay it down. Commit what's in your hand to the Father and watch what He does. His power combined with your obedience can result in unimaginable miracles!

And whatever you ask in prayer, you will receive,
if you have faith.
– (Matthew 21:22 ESV) –

CHAPTER THREE

IN HIS STRENGTH

I can do all things through Him who
strengthens me.

– (Philippians 4:13 NASB) –

Wwe were extremely grateful to the center which was kind enough to offer their stage and auditorium for us to produce our musical. We grew very attached to their staff and formed some lasting relationships. On the final night of the production, one of their workers approached me and asked where our school was going to be located. "I don't know yet," I responded. Looking a bit surprised, the young man exclaimed, "But I read in the paper where you are planning on opening in just a few weeks!" I smiled. "That's true," I responded. "I just don't know where." He chuckled and then asked what kind of facility we needed. "A little house would be ideal," I said. "We only have five students, so we don't need a lot of space." I went on to describe other details about the house we would need. As I spoke, he looked intrigued and then his face lit up. "You sound like you're describing a place we use for storage. Why don't you let me show it to you in the morning? You never know, the center might be willing to give it to you rent free for a couple of years."

The next morning, he met me in front of a tiny frame house. It was, at most, 700 square feet. Because they only used it for storage, there had been no reason for them to fix it up. Shrubs and trees were so overgrown it was a major effort just to access the front and back doors. The walls desperately needed to be patched and painted. Some of the tiles in the floors in a couple of the rooms were missing and the other floors were in great need of attention. Still, to us, this tiny facility was a thing of beauty! We were thrilled when we were given permission to move in and began pouring heart and soul into renovating this little house. In addition to fixing it up and cleaning up the yard around it, used furniture we had purchased needed to be painted, brochures needed to be designed and printed, and loads of other tasks needed to be done before opening our doors. There were volumes of paperwork and forms to be completed and filed. The days were long, and having my precious little one with me added still another dimension to my responsibilities. Thankfully, a young teenager who lived nearby was available to help keep an eye on her and keep her entertained while I feverishly worked to try and get everything done. In the evenings, after returning home, my phone rang incessantly with desperate parents on the other end of the line, anxious to hear when the center would open and how they could enroll their child.

Kristi, a lovely young woman who had just graduated from college, was hired to be our first teacher. After only a few short weeks of scrubbing and painting, raking and mowing, we hung a small wooden sign in front of the little frame house. On it were hand-painted letters that spelled out "The Little Light House." It was a dream come true when five adorable toddlers with special needs were carried through the door that day by their parents. They were greeted by their new teacher and five volunteers. It was October, 1972. That was our beginning.

I thought the days had been long before, but they proved to be easy compared to the days ahead. Because the mother of the other little girl who had shared my dream was pregnant and was unable to work full-time, it was determined I should serve as executive director to address the myriad of tasks that had to be done each day. There were policies and procedures which needed to be developed and letters that needed to be written, in addition to a host of other mounting duties. Many in the community had heard of our efforts, and so numerous calls began to pour in from good-hearted folks wanting to know how they could help as well as parents interested in enrolling their children. Each day brought more challenges and more tasks which I hadn't an inkling of how to accomplish. Even though we only offered classes two days a week, the young teacher and I were there each weekday and some Saturdays. The days were long and seventy-hour weeks weren't uncommon.

Within just a few months, I was physically, mentally, and emotionally exhausted. With no administrative experience under my belt, there was a learning curve to everything I tackled. I found myself feeling irritable, frustrated, and unable to cope. As time went on, these feelings evolved into a deep resentment. Why would God lead me into such a difficult endeavor? There were constant financial worries and a never-ending need for volunteers, equipment, and supplies. And then, of course, my first and foremost commitment as a wife and mother. How could I possibly do all that God seemed to be asking of me? It all seemed too much to deal with. These feelings seemed to escalate with every passing day and I was becoming hopelessly discouraged. I didn't know how long I could keep going.

I had noticed that Kristi remained calm and confident in the midst of it all. I marveled at her ability to handle such a heavy and overwhelming load even though she was fresh out of college. Every child had a different set of physical and mental challenges. Each had to have a program created just for him or her. The volunteers had to be trained. Teaching materials had to be created.

All the while she was having to manage with next-to-no budget and only the help of a few volunteers. All this, and yet she did it with a pervasive sense of peace about her. Nothing seemed to rattle her. Her mood was consistently optimistic. She always had a smile and a warm word for everyone. How did she do it? She was working just as long hours as I was. She had to feel just as overwhelmed. Within the first few months the number of students had doubled, even further diversifying the needs she was having to address. One child was blind, another had autism, and still another was blind with cerebral palsy. The list of special needs was as varied as the population of children who were enrolled. And each needed a very individualized, prescriptive program to maximize the most critical developmental years of their lives. Every child represented a whole set of goals and objectives and planned activities our young teacher had to write. She worked unbelievably hard, keeping up with the progress of each student and prescribing new activities each day as their needs changed. I couldn't wrap my mind around it. How was she managing it all? And beyond that, how did she do all she did with such a sense of peace?

I had noticed that every day at noon, Kristi would steal off into one of the classrooms and remain in there for thirty to forty-five minutes. She certainly had a right to a lunch break and so it had always been fine with me. After all, I had plenty of work to do and she deserved some quiet time of her own. But one day, more out of curiosity than anything, I knocked on the door of the little classroom where she seemed to hide away each day. She welcomed me to come in. When I did so, I was somewhat amused. There before me, sitting on one of the children's chairs, was our young teacher. Spread across one of the child-size tables was a thick loose-leaf Bible and some books. At her encouragement, I had a seat on one of the brightly-colored wooden chairs.

Hesitantly, I confessed I was just curious about what she did in the little room each day. She smiled and then gently explained. She said that Christ had given His all for her and she felt the least she could do was to give Him the center of her day. So each day for her lunch break, she spent time alone with Him. She told me

We can't carry out God-sized tasks without God-sized strength.

it was in this time alone with God that she gained her strength. I was fascinated. I had always loved the Lord, and had typically read a few verses out of the Bible each night and perhaps even a little devotional. But Kristi was literally studying the Bible, with pen and paper in hand. She had my complete attention as she described how she did this, making notes on what the Scriptures said, what they meant for her life, and what changes she would need to make in her life to apply those Scriptures and their principles.

From that day on, Kristi took me under her wing and escorted me into a whole new walk with God. That day was the beginning of my discipleship training. Only a few years younger than myself, she was wise way beyond her years. I learned volumes from her, but probably the most important Biblical principle I learned is that we can't carry out God-sized tasks without God-sized strength. In our own flesh, we don't have the strength to do what God calls us to do. We must rely on Him.

God had called me to a mission far beyond my capabilities. The same thing was true for our young teacher. And through her example, I began to understand my great need to rely on His supernatural strength and power. I began to go to Him each day, petitioning Him for all of our needs and asking Him to be my strength. Looking back now, I know that is the only way I made it through those difficult years. God was my strength!

Remarkably, some days I would write reports, draft charts, and complete any number of projects that I didn't know how to do. I would later look back and marvel at how God equipped me and taught me. He was my coach and my mentor. He was my comfort and my encourager. When I was physically depleted, He renewed my strength.

Years ago, I read a story about a priest who carried a tremendous amount of responsibility. So great was his load, his peers couldn't imagine him adding to it. Still, he was asked to lead a new effort, an enormous mission which would take up even more of his time. Those working with him were sure he would turn down the request. Yet after praying about it, he accepted. When asked how he could possibly add these new responsibilities to his load, he replied, "I'll simply have to spend another hour in prayer each morning."

Corrie Ten Boom illustrated this principle perfectly when she compared our lives to a glove:

> *The glove can do nothing. Oh, but if my hand is in the glove, it can do many things . . . cook, play the piano, write. Well, you say that is not the glove, but the hand in the glove that does it. Yes, that is so. I tell you that we are nothing but gloves. The hand in the glove is the Holy Spirit of God. Can the glove do something if it is very near the hand? No! The glove must be filled with the hand to do the work. That is exactly the same for us. We must be filled with the Holy Spirit to do the work God has for us to do.[3]*

For years to come, I would remember this powerful lesson and rely on our Heavenly Father to be my strength. For years to come, I would experience the truth of Corrie's "glove" illustration, and for years to come, I would witness God's faithfulness and His amazing ability to work through this weak vessel.

> *And the peace of God, which transcends all understanding, will guard your hearts and your minds in Christ Jesus.*
>
> – (Philippians 4:7 NIV) –

3. Corrie Ten Boom, *Each New Day* (Old Tappan, NJ: F. H. Revell, 1977), May 15 devotion.

CHAPTER FOUR

WHOM WILL YOU SERVE?

*No one can serve two masters, for either he will
hate the one and love the other, or he will be
devoted to the one and despise the other. You
cannot serve God and money.*

– (Mathew 6:24 ESV) –

Within nine months of opening our little school, the
student enrollment had tripled. The tiny house which
had so graciously been provided to us was no longer
adequate to meet our needs. We had committed early on to a
standard of one volunteer per child and with that ratio, we were
bulging at the seams.

By God's grace and amazing provision, a little over a year
after we opened our doors, a nearby church offered us space on
the third floor of their educational building. We enthusiastically
accepted their offer.

Financially, we were making it month to month, but just
barely. Many in the community had learned about our work and
we were blessed with in-kind donations as well as monetary gifts
which kept us afloat. We had hired a few additional staff members

to come alongside our one teacher, but we were desperately in need of therapists and additional teachers.

A short time after we settled into the church facilities, a public school official paid us a visit and approached me about an arrangement which he felt could be mutually beneficial to the school system as well as to the Little Light House.

Public Law 94-142 had been passed requiring public schools to provide "a free and appropriate public education" to every child with special needs.[4] A number of families had begun demanding that Tulsa Public Schools comply with the law.

At that time, the Tulsa public school system wasn't set up to accommodate the special needs of the families who were understandably insisting upon such services. So the chief administrator for the Special Education Department proposed to me that the Little Light House enter into a contractual agreement with Tulsa Public Schools. We would serve the children for whom the public school system was legally obligated to provide services, and they in turn would hire teachers and therapists to supplement our small staff and purchase some much-needed equipment for us. They explained that things would basically remain the same except our enrollment would increase and, as a matter of record, all Little Light House children would be placed on public school rolls as well as Little Light House rolls. All the students would attend "school" at our facility. The public school officials had been extremely impressed with our highly individualized program and were excited about the possibility of working together to meet the needs of these children. They presented the contract as a win/win proposition for everyone involved. There appeared to be so many positives, we felt the offer had to be a gift from God. So our Board of Directors approved the decision to move forward and sign the contract.

For three years, it was smooth sailing. Public school officials would frequently pay us visits, bring VIP guests through our facility, and express their pride in the program. All of the children benefitted from the additions to our professional team.

4. Education for All Handicapped Children Act of 1975, Public Law 94-192, Sec. 3 (c).

The families of the children seemed overjoyed to be receiving such quality, individualized services, the staff was thrilled to have additional team members, and the volunteer program was growing by leaps and bounds.

Over that three-year period, the Little Light House enrollment tripled and the entire program grew exponentially. One professional described our program as having experienced a ten-year growth within the first year and a half. Authorities in the field of special education even began referring to the Little Light House as a model program in a six-state region. Our dream had become a reality!

However, three years later, we were stunned when a small group of parents began questioning the "religious practices" of the Little Light House and demanded the public school investigate what they believed to be a conflict with separation of church and state laws. Early on, I had asked the officials if our Christian focus could ever be a problem. I was told not to worry about it. But after months of complaints and phone calls regarding the Bible stories we taught, the prayers in our classrooms, the Christian songs we sang, and the Bible posters on our walls, the public school officials felt they had no other alternative but to give the Little Light House an ultimatum. We were to either cease all "religious" practices or the public schools would be forced to sever all ties with the Little Light House and we would forfeit all public funds.

At that point, state funding constituted approximately seventy percent of the Little Light House budget and represented, from a human point of view, the only reliable source of income the ministry had.

We also were told if we did not comply with their demands, we would lose the majority of the students we served since they were technically on public school rolls (as well as ours). The program would be moved to a public facility, and that meant we could lose the majority of our staff as well. In a nutshell, it appeared that severing the contract would result in our pupil population dropping from thirty-six students to five, the loss of the majority of our staff, and the loss of most of our monetary income.

Faced with the impending deadline for a decision, the board members met far into the night. The membership was split. There were those who felt that failure to comply would mean certain death to the ministry which so many had poured their lifeblood into establishing. Others agreed but felt, no matter what, God had been responsible for turning a dream into a reality and for providing for the ministry; therefore, we couldn't turn our backs on Him now. After extensive prayer, discussion, and deliberation, the final decision of the majority was to turn down the demands of the public school officials, sever our contractual relationship with the state, and keep the Little Light House Christ-centered, regardless of the cost. That decision resulted in a tsunami-size testing of our faith.

A month later, ninety percent of the Little Light House student population had been transferred into a newly established program within a public school facility. Many parents went reluctantly, but did so out of concern the Little Light House doors would close. They felt they needed to ensure their child would have services. Also, out of fear the Little Light House would not survive, many of our staff accepted positions with public schools. Only a few staff members remained, each one uncompromisingly dedicated to the call of God on their lives to serve Him at the Little Light House at any cost. With so few students remaining, there was no need for the large volunteer corps we had attracted. So we thanked them for their service and most of them slowly drifted away and found other interests.

To the few staff and board members who remained, it was clear it would take an on-going series of twentieth-century miracles for the work of the Little Light House to continue. For each it was a test of their personal faith. Their decisions had been made purely out of obedience to our Almighty God and a deep love for the few children and families who remained. We explained to each staff member we had no idea if they would be paid on time or even if they'd have children in their classrooms.

The families whose children remained with us believed in the Little Light House and greatly valued the loving Christian atmosphere we offered, but even they were concerned about how the Little Light House could possibly survive. It seemed God was taking the entire ministry and everyone associated with it through a refiner's fire of sorts. It was a time of learning to trust God on a whole new level.

In the months that followed the split with the public school system, our remaining board and staff members fervently sought God's guidance. We clung to the words in Jeremiah 29:13 (NIV): *"You will seek me and find me when you seek me with all your heart."* And in the midst of the fire, we surely did just that! As we did, we heard His leading clearly. We were to restructure the entire corporate entity of the Little Light House, clearly identifying ourselves as a Christian Developmental Center for Children with Special Needs.

At the time of the founding, it had never even occurred to us to include the word Christian in the title or logo of our organization. God revealed to us that this had been a mistake. If we truly desired to keep Him at the helm, to operate by Biblical principles and to expose our children and families to His Word, His love, and His power in every possible way, we needed to be upfront about who and what we were. We were overwhelmed at the realization of all that needed to be done. In a sense, God was wanting to completely transform the Little Light House into a tuition-free ministry. It seemed overwhelming, but all those who remained involved were determined to yield to His guiding hand and allow the Almighty to reshape the Little Light House into the ministry He wanted it to be. The articles, bylaws, and all other corporate papers were rewritten. Every piece of Little Light House promotional literature was revised. A policy was put into place stating only followers of Christ would be eligible to come on our board or staff. We all needed to be committed to the same mission . . . that of bringing glory to our Lord, Jesus Christ.

Of course, our doors would be open to families regardless of their religious preferences, but they would know coming in, we incorporated prayer in our classrooms.

Christian songs would be sung and Bible stories read to the children. With no one controlling the purse strings, the Little Light House Board of Directors would be free to always listen to and obey our Heavenly Father regarding all matters.

We learned a valuable lesson through this experience. When we accepted state funding, we unknowingly put ourselves in a position of serving two masters. When we signed that contract, we committed to following their mandates and submitting to government rules and regulations which were inconsistent with what God was calling us to do.

All that glitters is not God!

Thankfully, in our nation, we have the freedom to follow God and to do His work, His way. We are at liberty to restrict our hiring to staff members who are totally devoted followers of Christ and to recruit only Christian board members. We are free to offer a Bible-rich curriculum and pray in our classrooms. In short, we have the blessed freedom to serve only one Master, our Heavenly Father, and do so without fear of consequences from our government.

Since those early years, there have been any number of other opportunities which looked, from the world's perspective, to be golden. However, in taking a closer look, we realized we would be putting ourselves in a position of attempting to serve two masters. Thankfully, the Little Light House remains committed to serving only one, our Lord Jesus Christ. May that always be!

There is an additional Biblical principle which goes hand-in-hand with serving only one master. It has to do with being equally yoked. While I have chosen not to devote an entire chapter to this subject, it is important to note that when we partner with those who do not share our core values and our faith in Christ Jesus, we are not in compliance with this key principle.

Years ago, I was teaching on serving only one master and referenced this principle of being equally yoked as well. After my lecture, a Little Light House staff member approached me and thanked me for my words. She said she and her husband had been struggling with a business partnership they had entered into years before. They had experienced great frustration, turmoil, and conflict in the relationship. She had realized as I spoke, they were unequally yoked with their business partners who were non-believers in the gospel of Christ. Hopefully, they were able to slip out of that partnership with their relationship intact. I'm sure they learned, through their difficult experience, to see the wisdom of God in this important Biblical principle.

As you hear the call to do God's work, I encourage you, be watchful of what might appear to be golden opportunities. All that glitters is not of God! Partner with those who share your commitment to Christ and embrace Biblical core values. Don't allow yourself to be drawn into any arrangement which yields control of your organization or efforts to anyone but your loving Heavenly Father.

> *Do not be bound together with unbelievers;*
> *for what partnership have righteousness and*
> *lawlessness, or what fellowship has light with*
> *darkness? Or what harmony has Christ with*
> *Belial, or what has a believer in common with an*
> *unbeliever?*
>
> – (2 Corinthians 6:14–15 NASB) –

CHAPTER FIVE
SHINE LIKE A LURE

*Let your light so shine before men, that they may
see your good works and glorify your Father
in heaven.*

– (Mathew 5:16 NKJV) –

During the time we were seeking God's guidance for restructuring the Little Light House, He consistently led us to Matthew 5:16. As we began to study this powerful Scripture in-depth, we discovered the heart of God's mission for all God's children. Wanting to preserve what we were learning, our staff and board did an intensive study of this Biblical truth. In the process, we uncovered insights which have served as a guiding force for the Little Light House ever since. It was to such a degree, we refer to Matthew 5:16 to this day as our Foundational Scripture.

Looking carefully at this mandate from God, He makes it plain to us that He has provided the power and the light. We must simply "*let*" His light shine through our lives. We don't have to do it in our own power. We simply need to be yielded and allow Him to work and shine through us. When Jesus was speaking these words to the multitudes, He was speaking to mankind. Whether we are applying His words to our lives personally or corporately, these words are for all of us to live by. They address what I believe our life's purpose should be.

The word *light* in this verse is referring to the light of His love and His gospel. We are to allow that light to be reflected in our lives. For those operating in His name, that means everything we do must reflect His Biblical standards as well as His loving power at work through us.

The word *so* in this Scripture is referencing to what degree our light is to shine. It is to be to such a great degree it attracts attention!

The word *shine* is defined by Webster's Dictionary as "to emit rays of light, to be bright by reflection of light, to be eminent, conspicuous, or distinguished, to be conspicuously evident or clear." When I think about the word shine in this Scripture, I'm reminded of a time when I was fishing on the banks of a beautiful mountain stream in Colorado. My eyes continued to be drawn to something shiny among some limbs on the other side of the stream. It obviously was reflecting the light of the sun and one couldn't help but notice it. I never did venture across the swift stream to check out exactly what it was (I suspect it was a metal lure that had become tangled on a limb), but I can recall wanting very much to be able to get closer to see exactly what was capturing my attention. I believe God desires our lives to be like that lure, causing our world to notice and want to check out the source of the light. When they do so, it should be our hope, they too will see a reflection—a reflection of the "Son," the Son of God.

As our light shines forth, the potential impact of our witness increases.

The *"men"* the Scripture refers to includes all people. At the Little Light House, we translate that to mean people from all walks of life. We are committed to allowing the light of God's gospel and love to shine forth to every parent, child, volunteer, constituent, deliveryman, repairman, or anyone who walks through our doors. A cup of cold water on a hot sunny day offered to someone like our mail carrier may very well be that glimmer of light needed to attract him or her into the saving, loving grace of Christ.

We believe the "*good works*" in this Scripture refers to the calling God places on our lives. At the Little Light House, we believe our calling is ministering to children with special needs as we help them develop to their maximum potential. The word *good* is indicating the works are to be carried out in such a way that His love and power are reflected and God is glorified.

God has a good work for each and every one of us. That good work is the means by which we are to fulfill His purpose for our lives. I believe this is true for corporate bodies as well. Whether you are reading this as an individual, the head of a corporation, church, or small business, God has a specific work for you to do. Not only that, He wants you to do it in such a way that people are drawn to your work and will want to know more about God as a result.

Therefore, at the Little Light House, our ultimate goal is to do what God has called us to do in such a way, the attention of our world is drawn to God and He is glorified. This sets the standard for all areas of operation and disallows decisions which would compromise the witness of the Little Light House for our Lord and Savior, Jesus Christ.

There are few news reports that are more disheartening to me than those covering ministries or Christian businesses which have failed to pay their bills and/or taxes or whose leaders have been caught in adulterous affairs, embezzlement, or other such grievous transgressions. Sadly, such reports cause many to stumble, and even question their faith. I want to be careful here, because I am not sitting in judgment of those who have been the victims of the enemy's schemes. I understand we live in a fallen world and all of us commit sins. I also recognize God can bring good out of our mistakes. Romans 8:28 (ESV) reads: *"And we know that for those who love God all things work together for good, for those who are called according to his purpose."* Of that there is no question. At the same time, we all need to recognize that as Christians, we have a responsibility to God to be uncompromisingly committed to maintaining a positive witness for Christ. Our world is watching. Our light must shine!

Matthew 5:16 beautifully outlines this calling and this responsibility. As our light shines forth, the potential impact of our witness increases. If we do not abide by Biblical standards, our witness can have the reverse effect and turn people away from our Master and Savior.

As we yield our lives to Him (and our businesses, schools, churches, and organizations), He is faithful to give us the strength to resist the spiritual forces of darkness. As we rely on that supernatural strength, we will be able to do the work He has called us to do in a way that brings Him glory and honor, thus drawing our world to want to take a closer look. When they do, may they be drawn into the healing grace and love of our Savior, Jesus Christ.

You are the light of the world. A city set on a hill cannot be hidden.

− (Matthew 5:14 ESV) −

CHAPTER SIX
DEATH OF A VISION

I tell you the truth, unless a kernel of wheat is
planted in the soil and dies, it remains alone.
But its death will produce many new kernels—a
plentiful harvest of new lives.

– (John 12:24 NLT) –

Looking back on the events and trials of the two-year period following the split with the public school system, it is easy to see now what God was doing. However, in the midst of it, we were all left feeling hurt, confused, and emotionally and even spiritually depleted. Lasting from 1976 to 1978, it was the most trying and difficult season in the Little Light House history. Perhaps the most crushing blow was the persecution which came from a handful of parents who had hoped we would comply with the demands of the state. Many of the parents were emotionally devastated by the challenges which come along with raising a child with special needs. Many were angry with God and the last thing they wanted was to hear about God at the school they took their child to each day. They were struggling emotionally and spiritually and needed a scapegoat. Unfortunately, we were it.

There were some donors who turned against us as well. They were unhappy with the fact that the Little Light House had been restructured and more clearly defined as a Christian Developmental Center. One contributor returned his monthly Little Light House newsletter. With a bold red magic marker, he had circled the word Christian at the top of the newsletter. Above it, he wrote one word: "WHY?!"

Countless other supporters in the community assumed the ministry had closed. It was easy to understand why. The sudden drop in enrollment, the lack of funds, the loss of board members, staff members, and volunteers all painted a bleak and hopeless picture. From all indications, the ministry appeared dead. The vision we believed so strongly the Lord had given to us seemed to have died with it.

God sometimes allows a vision to die so that He can resurrect it in new form.

The whole experience knocked the spiritual props out from under me. There seemed no reason to go on. I had never known such despair. At times, as a founder and executive director, I wanted desperately to throw in the towel. I felt beaten up and even abandoned by God. Where was the ever-loving, all powerful God who had demonstrated His miracle-working power over and again in the early days of the Little Light House? How could He let the vision He had given us die?

One evening, the dam of emotions gave way. I cried all the way home and fell into bed in a state of complete exhaustion. Two young staff members who had been my greatest support sensed I had reached a breaking point. That evening they came to my house. My husband led them back to the dark bedroom where I had been since I arrived home. Seeing them brought even more tears as I poured out my heart to them. I told them I didn't think I could go on. I felt I had nothing left to give. My strength was completely depleted. It was that night I was first introduced to a concept which one can find repeated throughout Biblical history. My young friends referred to it as "death of a vision." They explained that oftentimes God allows a vision to die so that He can resurrect it in a new form, making it into more of what He wants it to be so that it will ultimately reflect His power and bring Him glory.

Pastor Cecil Thompson addressed the concept of death of a vision in this way:

> We are all fired up when the vision is fresh and new, but almost without warning things explode. Instead of seeing our vision fulfilled, it is like death has destroyed the vision . . . Joseph had a vision of being a son that was honored by his brothers. The death of his vision was being sold into slavery, falsely accused, thrown into a prison, and forgotten by Pharaoh's butler, who had made a promise to mention his false imprisonment. It was like he experienced death after death. There is a truth that rings loud and clear . . . It is not the end!!! . . . In the lives of God's precious people there will be shattered dreams and the death of a vision. This is almost a certainty. Perhaps the only time we will not encounter them is when we have no vision in the first place.[5]

That night as my sweet friends and coworkers sat on the bed with me, they prayed and then said some words I'll never forget—words that prompted me to want to hang on and even gave me hope that God was going to do great things. "Marcia, we understand from a human point of view, it does look like a death to the Little Light House dream and vision. We also understand how tired you are, and how and why you might want to give up. You can give up if you want. You can walk away. But we believe God isn't finished with the Little Light House. We believe when God's involved, after a death comes a resurrection, and we would just hate for you not to be around when God resurrects the Little

---

Light House!" I felt in my heart of hearts they were right. I'm sure as a result of their prayers and those of many saints, my spirits were lifted and I committed to continuing on as long as God could use me.

Times remained hard, however, and there were moments I wondered if it was time for me to suggest to the Little Light House Board of Directors that we close our doors. Yet, inevitably, in those moments, God would send a sign or encourage my heart to keep believing, keep trusting, and wait on Him.

His encouragement would come in different forms. One of the few students we still had enrolled would experience a miraculous milestone. A parent would stop by to express their gratitude for the Little Light House, or a contributor would send an uplifting note or an unusually large gift. Whatever form it came in, God had a way of impressing upon my heart that we were to persevere and trust Him.

In the midst of it all, God united the hearts of the few staff members who had remained. In the most excruciatingly difficult moments, we encouraged one another in the faith. During a particularly painful period, one staff member described what we were going through by saying, "When we took a strong stand to remain a Christian center, it was as though we threw sand in Satan's face and expected him to lie down and play dead. He didn't!" Without question, we were under grave spiritual attack in those days. The spiritual enemy would have loved for us to have given up.

Slowly but surely, however, new families of children with special needs began to make their way to our door. These were families who were seeking quality services, and were grateful to find such services in a Christ-centered environment.

As the enrollment steadily increased, the volunteers likewise began to return. Churches and other believers heard of the stand our ministry had taken for Christ and began to send additional financial support and in-kind donations.

By 1979, the Little Light House was at maximum capacity again. As we trusted Him, God had been faithful to bring us through His refiner's fire. In the process, He purged and transformed the ministry and the hearts of everyone involved. Every aspect of the Little Light House had been reshaped and redefined. Every member of our board and staff had also experienced God in a new way.

When gold is left on the fire long enough, the dross (or the impurities) can be raked off and what will be left is pure gold. It is only then the refiner can peer into the glimmering gold and see a clear reflection of himself.

I believe God allowed the ministry and each of us personally to go through His refiner's fire so that He could purge and sculpt the Little Light House into the ministry He needed it to be for the future. He knew for the Little Light House to be a light to the world and a model training center on a global scale, it had to become a true reflection of Him and His love.

Was it painful? Oh my, yes! Was it long and hard? Without question! Would I go through it all over again in order for God to have the outcome He desired? In a heartbeat! On the other side of it, our hearts had been changed and we each found ourselves stronger in Christ with a clearer understanding of the work God had called us to carry out.

I believe every ministry or Christian business must be willing to go through God's refiner's fire and perhaps even a death of a vision. In the midst of such times, we each individually and corporately must trust God. We must know He is working for our good and His ultimate glory, to mold and shape and create (and, in some cases, re-create) a ministry which is a true reflection of Himself.

Silver and gold are purified by fire, but God
purifies hearts.

– (Proverbs 17:3 TLB) –

Trust in the LORD with all your heart, and lean not on your own understanding; in all your ways acknowledge Him and He will direct your paths.

– (Proverbs 3:5-6 MEV) –

CHAPTER SEVEN
TRUST AND TRANSFORMATION

And do not be conformed to this world, but be transformed by the renewing of your mind, so that you may prove what the will of God is, that which is good and acceptable and perfect.

– (Romans 12:2 NSAB) –

One of most unique ways we grew and developed was the result of a decision of our staff members who unanimously agreed on a rather unorthodox policy. The policy stated the Little Light House would always pay the ministry's bills first and pay our staff with whatever was left over. Each staff member felt they had made a commitment to the Lord to be a part of the Little Light House ministry and they would trust Him for their provisions. They based their decision on God's promise in Philippians 4:19 (NASB), *"And my God shall supply all your needs according to His riches in glory in Christ Jesus."* At the time, to our knowledge, there were no federal laws to prohibit a voluntary commitment to delay receipt of a paycheck.

So for decades, staff members voluntarily did exactly that. When finances got tight, they voluntarily gave up timely receipt of their paychecks, as they were able, some waiting up to seven payroll periods to be paid. Miraculously, everyone was always eventually paid in full. During those difficult but ministry-forming years, lives were dramatically impacted and amazing transformations took place. I especially recall the joy the staff exuded as they went about their work. If parents, volunteers, or constituents happened to learn that staff members were voluntarily going without their paychecks, they were always surprised and amazed. Nothing about the demeanor of our staff revealed the sacrifices they were making for the mission of the Little Light House. The witness was powerful!

During one particular season when the majority of our staff had been voluntarily delaying receipt of their paycheck for an especially long time, one staff member cheerfully proposed that we begin a staff commune grocery exchange system. She shared a Scripture that God had impressed upon her heart. It was Acts 4:32 (NIV): "*All the believers were one in heart and mind. No one claimed that any of their possessions was their own, but they shared everything they had.*" She went on to suggest that each morning when we gathered for prayer and devotions, we should circulate a legal pad. Each staff member would use it to list any item they had need of but didn't have the funds to purchase at the time. The staff enthusiastically agreed and the unusual practice began.

Paper towels, toothpaste, deodorant, flour, sugar . . . the list was varied and often long. Once complete, it was posted and the next day, staff members who happened to have extra of the listed items would bring them to share with the staff who needed them. Staff members marveled at how God not only met their most basic needs, but increased their faith and deepened their love for one another at the same time. This was a transformation they experienced which may not have happened any other way but God's way.

My husband, Phil, also experienced God's transformative power not long after the ministry was established. Being in the finance business, he was acutely sensitive to the financial needs of the ministry. Though he had never been a worrier, he found himself feeling increasingly stressed about the financial obligations of the ministry. His anxiety peaked one particular month as he perseverated over a bill for $1,200 that was about to come due. The coffers were running unusually low and from a human point of view, there seemed no way we would be able to pay it. "We just can't keep operating this way," Phil lamented one afternoon. "We never know where the money is going to come from!" He stewed far into the night and for a couple of days more. But the next day he walked into the living room with a sheepish expression on his face. He then handed me a check made out to the Little Light House which had been delivered that day. It was from a local civic club. They had decided to begin supporting the Little Light House and were committing to a pledge of $200 a month for the next year. They also had decided to make it six months retroactive. So the check Phil held in his hand was made out for $1,200, the exact amount we needed, to the penny!

I'll never forget the expression on his face as he quietly uttered the words, "I'll never doubt again." Phil's words are etched in my memory to this day. And though he would quickly admit there certainly were times after that day which tested his faith,

When doing God's work, God's way, we can expect to experience transformation.

without question, that moment transformed him spiritually. His trust became deeper and his walk with the Lord closer.

Denise, a long-time volunteer and dedicated Little Light House board member, has another transformation story which she experienced years ago while serving on staff at the Little Light House. It was during a time when she was one who had voluntarily sacrificed timely receipt of her paycheck for several pay periods. Her child's birthday was approaching and plans had long been in place for an extra-special celebration. As the day drew closer, Denise realized there was no way financially she could throw the party her child had dreamed of which she had lovingly planned to do. In fact, there wasn't even money for a cake. She gave the matter to God and what transpired after that can only be explained as God's divine provision. In perfect timing, tickets to a brand-new amusement park just happened to be donated to the Little Light House for use by anyone on staff. Everyone quickly agreed they should be used for the child's birthday. Then, a staff member who had once worked in a bakery offered to decorate a birthday cake for the child. Overnight, a fabulous birthday party came together on a far more grandiose scale than anyone could have imagined! In reflecting on this amazing gift from God, Denise would tell you it impacted her spiritual life forever and transformed her into one who trusts God for all her day-to-day needs.

As we trust God and see Him bless us, our lives are constantly impacted and hearts continue to be transformed. As Christians and especially as ministry leaders, we can expect transformation as we do the work of the Lord in the way He would have us do it. As we trust, our faith is stretched, our prayer life is strengthened, and our hearts draw closer and closer to our Lord, our Provider, and our Savior, Jesus Christ.

Therefore, if anyone is in Christ, he is a new creation. The old has passed away; behold, the new has come.

– (2 Corinthians 5:17 ESV) –

CHAPTER EIGHT

MEDIOCRITY DOESN'T SHINE!

*So whether you eat or drink or whatever you do,
do it all for the glory of God.*

– (1 Corinthians 10:31 NIV) –

As we trusted God, we followed His lead into a greater understanding of the ramifications for our mission of our foundational Scripture, Matthew 5:16. God took us deeper into the meaning of words such as "good works" which meant more than just doing the work He had called us to do. It even meant more than carrying out the works in a way that reflected His Biblical principles and offered a positive witness for Him. Slowly but surely, we began to see that in order for our work with these precious children and their families to shine like the fishing lure in that Colorado mountain stream, it had to represent excellence of the highest degree. No one is attracted to mediocrity. It simply doesn't shine!

It was also through Matthew 5:16 God began to unfold a new vision for our leadership. God was calling the Little Light House to model excellence to such a degree, people would be drawn from around the world to gain new insights into working with

> *To fulfill this new calling, we would not only need to shine, we would need to be radiant.*

children with special needs. He was slowly but surely shaping the Little Light House into a model training center. Our classrooms were to become a classroom to our world.

To fulfill this new calling, we would not only need to shine, we would need to be radiant! This meant our standards had to be significantly above the norm. The very name of the Little Light House would need to represent a benchmark of quality and excellence. Every aspect of the ministry would need to reflect a commitment to going above and beyond in the way we minister to children with special needs and their families.

God led us to look at every component of the ministry: how we answer the phone, how we greet each person who walks through the door, and even how we interact with each other. We all realized commitment to excellence in every arena was the only way the ministry would ever become a model center. We knew, too, God was calling us not only to a corporate commitment but an individual commitment to excellence as well.

The challenge was great. Working with a zero budget, relying on donations, and managing a staff without the benefit of the most competitive wages are factors which might make such a goal seem impossible. It called for trust, trust in the Almighty to guide us and provide for us. He didn't let us down.

From the very beginning, God raised up remarkably gifted and dedicated staff members with exceptional expertise to help respond to this extremely high calling. They set high standards in all areas of the ministry. They were individuals who were first and foremost devoted to His service and furthering the kingdom of God. They caught the vision for the model of excellence God wanted the Little Light House to be and they worked diligently toward that end.

Over the years, we have fallen short many times and in many

ways, but it blesses me to say that overall the name of the Little Light House has come to reflect a commitment to excellence. God continues to bless us with staff who share that same vision. Our children's services staff members dedicate themselves to ensuring each child has a highly individualized, prescriptive program. Our volunteer coordinator is committed to providing quality training for our volunteers.

Professional conferences hosted by the Little Light House are carefully planned to make certain every element of the event is first-rate. Vigorous preparation goes into ensuring registration is organized and runs smoothly. Refreshments are presented in an attractive and appealing manner. Speakers receive the red-carpet treatment, a gift, and any assistance they may need.

We've been blessed with outstanding development staff members who meticulously plan out every detail of each fund-raising event we conduct. Following each event, a debriefing is held to analyze how the event can be improved upon the following year. Our administrative team must be equally as committed to reflecting excellence whether it is in the correspondence we send out, the effectiveness of our in-house communications, or the promptness of acknowledging donations.

Living up to this standard must be an on-going effort, and there are always areas which we are painfully aware of that need to be shored up as we strive to remain faithful. We fall and we fail, but knowing our divine calling keeps us focused.

As we have pursued excellence, God has been at work on a global scale orchestrating divine connections which have led to increased opportunities to impact children around the world. As a result, over the past two decades, we have welcomed scores of international interns representing eleven countries to come and study with us. Our staff has been invited to conduct seminars and training symposiums in Russia, China, Estonia, Kenya, Costa Rica, the Philippines, Mexico, Pakistan, Haiti, Ecuador, Honduras, and Hawaii. Forty-eight delegations from thirty-six nations have visited and toured the Little Light House. When they come, they are looking to see the highest standards. In addition, the Little Light House, Central Mississippi (a Little Light House affiliate established in 2006), also relies on the Tulsa model for training and guidance. It brings me great joy to know that as people from across the globe are being drawn to the work of the Little Light House, they are being exposed to the shining light of the gospel of Christ.

The Little Light House call to excellence has never been stronger than it is today. At the time of this writing, more than a thousand college and university students are relying on our center for practicums, internships, and observation experiences each year. They are counting on the Little Light House to reflect an ideal learning environment for the children we serve.

There is a call to standards of excellence on every ministry and, for that matter, every entity presenting itself as Christian and representing our Lord, Jesus Christ. For as that excellence shines forth, God is glorified. And as Christians, that, my friends, must be our mission.

Show yourself in all respects to be a model of good works, and in your teaching show integrity, dignity, and sound speech that cannot be condemned, so that an opponent may be put to shame, having nothing evil to say about us.

– (Titus 2:7-8 ESV) –

CHAPTER NINE

"WHO ME?"

*Each time he said, "No. But I am with you; that
is all you need. My power shows up best in weak
people." Now I am glad to boast about how weak
I am; I am glad to be a living demonstration of
Christ's power, instead of showing off my own
power and abilities.*

– (2 Corinthians 12:9 TLB) –

I knew the task was going to be challenging; in fact, some
might even say daunting. Our Little Light House Board
of Directors had charged me with the task of selecting an
architect to design our first state-of-the-art, 20,000-square-foot
permanent homesite. It was 1988. Prior to that time, we had been
housed in "borrowed" church space. For eighteen years we had
transformed the areas used for Sunday school into Little Light
House classrooms every Monday morning. The transformation
involved taking down all the church furniture and setting up our
own equipment and supplies. At one time, we were taking down
over 150 folding chairs and placing them in a storage room. On
Fridays, we did the same thing in reverse to prepare the space

for church use that weekend. A beautiful space of our own had been a long-time dream and it was finally becoming a reality. We wanted to get it right. After all, this was God's ministry and we desired everything about it to be to His glory. Selecting the right architect was critical to making our dream center all we needed it to be.

The Board of Directors had narrowed the choices down to three architectural firms and I had prepared a list of questions for them. When the day for the interviews finally arrived, the first architect was ushered into my office. The distinguished-looking gentleman greeted me with a firm, enthusiastic handshake. His starched shirt, coat, and tie matched his positive air of confidence. After the usual pleasantries, we got down to business. Without missing a beat, the seasoned professional told me all about his firm, how long they'd been in existence, and other pertinent information about his team. His presentation was impressive to say the least. Finally, it was time for me to ask what I believed was the most important question. "Can you tell me, what qualifies you to design a facility as unique as the Little Light House permanent homesite needs to be?" He smiled broadly. "Why of course!" With that he pulled from his portfolio any number of glossy photos of architectural projects which had been designed by his firm. There were many and they were diversified. He assured me his firm was more than qualified. I smiled and thanked him for his time.

The second gentleman was a mirror reflection of the first. And then it was time for the third interview. A kindly-looking man named Jim greeted me warmly as he stepped inside my office. We knew each other faintly through a mutual friend. He sat down, and looking very uncomfortable, he loosened the tie he was wearing. He chuckled softly and mumbled something about not typically wearing a tie.

He expressed appreciation for the opportunity to be considered for the job. In a very humble manner, he shared a bit about his firm and then I asked him the same question I had asked the others. "Jim, tell me, what do you feel you have done that uniquely qualifies you to design such a one-of-a-kind facility as is needed for the Little Light House?" Jim thought for a moment and then smiled and shook his head. "You know, my boss would not be happy with me for saying this, but honestly I'm not sure we have done anything that would qualify us for a project as special as this. This is God's ministry and God's project and well . . . I'd have to be on my knees every step of the way!"

In that very moment, I knew God was speaking to my heart. This humble man was God's chosen one for the job. I knew without question, though he was a gifted and experienced architect, he wouldn't be depending on his own knowledge. Rather, he would be depending on God as his source of strength, insight, and creativity. The project was awarded to his firm and we never regretted it. They designed a facility which served as an ideal setting for the next two and a half decades until we needed more space.

Some might have looked at all those I interviewed and considered Jim the least likely candidate and I would have to agree, from a human point of view. But, from God's perspective, he was the perfect choice. You see, since Biblical times, the least likely have been the very ones God has chosen time and again to carry out His greatest missions. Mary was just an innocent young girl when the angel Gabriel appeared to her telling her she was going to be the mother of the Christ-child. Joseph was just a poor carpenter, yet he was chosen to be Mary's husband and the earthly father to Jesus. David was just a young shepherd boy, yet he was chosen to be king of all of Israel. Peter was just a fisherman, yet was chosen to be a part of Jesus' inner circle.

Time and again throughout the Scriptures, we see God using ordinary people, people of no great influence, wealth, or education, yet they all had one thing in common: a heart for God and a willingness to be used by God. Each one felt inadequate for the task. Each expressed their dependence on God and as a result of their reliance on Him, their lives impacted millions. In many cases, they changed history.

Likely, when each was approached about their mission or calling, their first reaction was, "Who? Me? Are you kidding?!" I know that was certainly my reaction when God first began impressing upon my heart to begin a school for children with special needs. As I shared in previous chapters, both the cofounder and I were young housewives with no administrative experience or knowledge. Like so many others God has called to a challenging mission, we had no distinctive qualifications, no influence in our community, no special skills, and most assuredly no confidence in ourselves to accomplish such a task. Likewise, our first young teacher had barely completed her student teaching experience when she accepted the job. Yet, she created a unique and highly individualized approach to special education that is still utilized by the Little Light House more than four decades later.

Often the least likely are the very ones God calls to carry out His greatest missions.

God in His grace and mercy sees our hearts. He knows full well how inadequate each of us is for the task, but He also knows as we rely on Him, His strength and power will be sufficient and He will be glorified. For years, when I interviewed highly credentialed applicants for positions at the Little Light House, it was music to my ears when I would hear them acknowledge their inadequacies and express their dependence on God.

Oh, don't get me wrong. Our staff members are all exceptionally qualified. They must be for accreditation purposes. But even with college degrees and state-required licenses, our teachers and therapists are quick to say they rely on the Lord for real insight on how to most effectively help our children. In more than forty years, I never heard a teacher say their college training had adequately prepared them for the complex needs of the students at the Little Light House. Each one will readily express their dependence on God to help them effectively minister to the children we serve who have so many and such diverse needs.

A story one of our physical therapists shares about an experience she had on a mission trip serves as a classic illustration of this point. While ministering at an orphanage in China, Linda found herself completely at a loss to know how to help a little girl with cerebral palsy. The child sat with her arms seemingly locked behind her back and refused to let anyone touch her arms or hands. Linda knew they couldn't help this child under such conditions. That night, she went to our Heavenly Father and petitioned Him for help, acknowledging that even with over two decades of experience as a physical therapist, nothing had prepared her to help this child. The next morning God impressed upon her heart to ask the team if anyone happened to have brought any bright fingernail polish on the trip with them (not an item commonly packed for a mission trip). Amazingly, one team member had not one but several bottles of shiny fingernail polish—vibrant red fingernail polish, no less! When they approached the children that morning, they showed them the polish and offered to paint their fingernails. The children squealed with delight and clamored to have their nails done. Even the little boys wanted in on the action. As they put the fingernail polish on the children, they couldn't help but notice the child who previously would not let anyone touch her. Though she couldn't speak, she was now doing everything possible to draw attention to herself. Once she had their attention, she ever so slowly began to painstakingly pour all her efforts into moving her arms to her lap so her fingernails, too, could be painted bright red. Qualified and credentialed as she was, Linda was acutely aware of her need for a divine consult. She sought the wisdom of her Heavenly Father and, as a result, she made a dramatic difference in the life of a child.

When we are self-reliant, we are far more likely to accept the credit for our accomplishments, failing to give God the glory. However, as we recognize our need for Him and rely on His power and strength to work within us, missions are fulfilled and lives are changed.

*On behalf of such a man I will boast; but on my
own behalf I will not boast,
except in regard to my weaknesses.*

– (2 Corinthians 12:5 NASB) –

CHAPTER TEN

POTENTIAL TO BLOSSOM

*As Jesus was walking along, he saw a man who
had been blind from birth. "Rabbi," his disciples
asked him, "why was this man born blind? Was
it because of his own sins or his parents' sins?" "It
was not because of his sins or his parents' sins,"
Jesus answered. "This happened so the power of
God could be seen in him."*

– (John 9:1-3 NLT) –

I knew the question would come. Quite frankly I had hoped it might fall to my husband. But I knew that was not to be one evening as I was in bed catching up on some reading. My sixteen-year-old daughter plopped down at the end of the bed and, with tears streaming down her face, choked out the words . . . "Why?! Mom, I just want to know why!" With that, a dam of emotions broke and the sobs came in waves.

I had been expecting it. All of her friends were getting their driver's license. The talk at school seemed to always turn to who had finally passed their driver's test or who had a new car. Being legally blind since birth, our daughter, Missy, had been told by doctors, in no uncertain terms, she would never drive.

She had endured the teasing because of the glasses she wore in elementary school. She had dealt with the challenges day-to-day life brings to someone whose sight is impaired. She had even been willing to spend twice as long as other kids on her school work due to her visual limitations. But this was too much! She had finally reached a breaking point and was demanding an answer to an age-old question that has been voiced again and again since the beginning of time. "Why?"

It seems like such a simple question, but theologians have been debating the answer for centuries. Now, my beautiful young daughter sat before me, demanding an answer. I breathed a prayer, asking God for wisdom and guidance.

"Darlin'," I softly began, "you can ask why for the rest of your life, and it will only lead to pain and despair. But if you will turn your thinking around and ask God how, how He can use the circumstances of your life for good, you will find joy and victory! Romans 8:28 reads, '*And all these things work together for good for those who love the Lord and are called according to His purpose.*' As you trust Him and let Him guide you, He will work through your life and use you for His glory."

We talked long into the night and finally, exhausted, she returned to her own bed. Later, she shared with her father and me that months prior to that evening, she had become bitter toward God and had even stopped praying. But that night, she went running back to her Heavenly Father and His arms were open wide to her. It was soon after that God began opening doors for her music ministry. Over the next ten years, she traveled all over the nation sharing her testimony in concert, encouraging others facing difficult circumstances to ask how, not why.

As I mentioned, Missy wasn't the first to ask "Why?" John 9:1 tells of a time the disciples were walking along and saw a man who was born blind. They asked Jesus why this had happened. "Was it a result of his own sins or those of his parents?" And Jesus answered them, saying, "Neither, but that the power of God be manifested." Through Missy's visual impairment as a child, God inspired a ministry to children with special needs and then demonstrated His power, love, and provision in ways that could only be described as miraculous over the next four decades.

Children with special needs have a way of reaching the seemingly unreachable parts of our souls.

Over the years, I have observed endless numbers of children and adults with special needs whom God has worked through to impact their world. Parents have become stronger and more patient. Neighbors and relatives have become kinder and incalculable numbers of those who come in contact with these children speak of becoming more sensitive to the things of God.

In my book, *Milestones & Miracles*, I included an article written by a father of a little girl who came into the world with numerous physical challenges. She lived a very short life yet she impacted the heart and life of everyone who came in contact with her. Her father summed up her life this way:

> *Could a sightless, wordless, helpless infant ever be successful in ministry? If success is fulfilling God's purposes, I consider Mandy wildly successful. Can a ministry that's cut short be blessed by God? Mandy's earthly ministry lasted less than two years, but it touched eternity. And I suspect that's where real success is measured.*[6]

If we only have hearts to listen, children with special needs have a way of reaching the seemingly unreachable parts of our soul. They teach us lessons we can't learn any other way. David

---

6. Article by Marshall Shelley, editor of *Leadership Journal*, in Marcia Mitchell's *Milestones & Miracles* (Tulsa, OK: Little Light House, 1993), 80.

Glover, founder of P.U.R.E. ministries, explained it well when he said,

> *Unbeknownst to them, PURE people (people with special needs) have a unique ability to teach us profound truth. They don't sit us down and preach to us, for many can't speak. They don't pridefully say, 'Follow me,' for many can't walk. They don't say, 'Watch me,' for many have never even seen themselves. But in their usual quiet, unassuming way of living, they change us—if we let them.[7]*

David Glover is so right! They will not only teach us, they will inspire us. But we must be careful not to limit their dreams or fail to recognize their potential.

In a PowerPoint presentation I delivered to a number of developing nations, I shared illustrations of individuals with special needs who, because they had someone believing in them, defied the odds and accomplished their goals. I included Helen Keller, born profoundly hearing impaired and totally blind, who became a college-educated author and lecturer. I also spoke about a young man with Down syndrome who became a famous actor, a young woman without arms who became a pilot, and two magnificent ballet dancers who performed together, one of whom was missing an arm and the other a leg.

At the close of a training conference we were conducting in Fuzhou City, China, we invited participants to the microphone for questions or comments. One sweet lady stepped up to the microphone and, through a translator, quietly spoke these words. "Where I come from, we have always seen these children as," she hesitated, "as trouble." She continued, "But after hearing your teaching, we now see them as flowers with potential to blossom." There was hardly a dry eye among our team members. She got it! And hopefully, hundreds of others had also grasped the value these children bring to our world.

---

7. David Glover, *A Better Way: Where Least Is Most* (Bloomington, IN: WestBow Press, 2016), 290.

We never know just how much "potential to blossom" these children have, but at the Little Light House we believe each child deserves the opportunity to develop to his or her maximum potential, whatever that is. It is up to us to find the key to unlock the hidden treasure within each child.

There is no greater example of what I'm talking about than a little boy who was brought to the Little Light House years ago. He was just a toddler when he was first enrolled, had no use of his arms or legs, and was unable to speak. He could not use sign language as a result of limited use of his hands.

We didn't know the potential locked within this little one, but like with so many others, our teachers and therapists set out to find the key. They did. Following two years of working with this little guy, he was able to begin communicating for the first time in his life with the help of a device which was calibrated to his eyes. By the age of eleven, this same little guy had become CEO of his own company and was receiving numerous awards for his entrepreneurial spirit. Keith started out with a simple lemonade stand, but then set his sights on raising $120,000 for the Little Light House. He wanted to give back to the school that had made such a difference in his life. He met his goal and established the Keith Boyd Foundation for the purpose of raising money to get other boys and girls like himself the kinds of communication devices which have so greatly helped him. We never know the impact these children may have on their world.

A parent of a Little Light House child said it beautifully. "Liam is my daily teacher, and I wouldn't understand love and compassion if it weren't for his pure innocence." This is the kind of statement I've heard from countless parents of children with special needs over the years. Without question, without ever knowing it or even intending to do so, they touch our lives in amazing and unexpected ways.

One of my favorite stories reportedly took place at a Special Olympics track event years ago. The starting gun was sounded and the young runners took off. A short way down the track, however, one little competitor took a tumble and fell. Two of his running buddies noticed him go down hard. Despite the shouts of the crowd to keep running toward the finish line, they turned and began running in the opposite direction toward their young friend. One by one, each of the special athletes came to the aid of their buddy. Together they helped him to his feet and, once assured he was alright, they all linked arms and with faces beaming, proudly crossed the finish line together. Without a word, these young athletes had stirred the hearts of every spectator in the stands.

It never ceases to amaze me how children like these impact the world around them. We witness it every day at the Little Light House. In fact, it is rather ironic; we are supposed to be helping them reach their maximum potential, but in truth, they are the ones helping us to reach ours.

Whether you're relating to your employer, neighbor, business associate, family member, or customer, these children serve as a model to us. They exemplify how we are to respond to our world. They show us how to see each other from God's perspective and love each other with His unconditional love.

People were bringing even infants to him that he might touch them; and when the disciples saw it, they sternly ordered them not to do it. But Jesus called for them and said, "Let the little children come to me, and do not stop them; for it is to such as these that the kingdom of God belongs. Truly I tell you, whoever does not receive the kingdom of God as a little child will never enter it."

– (Luke 18:15-17 NRSV) –

CHAPTER ELEVEN

ENTERTAINING ANGELS

For I was hungry and you gave me food, I was
thirsty and you gave me drink,
I was a stranger and you welcomed me.

– (Matthew 25:35 ESV) –

We need only look to Scripture to discover the myriad of ways we are called to live out our potential to let God's love shine forth to a hurting world. In Hebrews 13:2 (ESV) we are told not to *"neglect to show hospitality to strangers, for thereby some have entertained angels unawares."* God is reminding us we are to show hospitality to each and every one who passes our way whether we know them or not.

Numerous times throughout the decades, our Little Light House staff has struggled with this principle, trying to understand how to balance workload and God's call to hospitality. The Greek word for "hospitality" in the New Testament in its literal translation means "love of strangers." That may seem like a tall order, but we have come to the conclusion, in ministry, it is God's order and one we must embrace. The challenge is, there is always so much to do, deadlines to be met, meetings to conduct, and projects to complete. It's difficult to get it all done, yet show God's kindness to all who enter. In a non-profit like the Little Light House, we have many visitors who stop by to drop off donations, make deliveries, inquire about the services we offer, and a host of other reasons.

As blessed as we are by each guest and as glad as we are to see each one, our staff members often feel pulled due to ever-increasing workloads. Still, the mandate is the same—to always show hospitality. Our figurative welcome mat is always to be out and, be it a foundation representative or an eight-year-old Girl Scout, each guest should sense they are important and valued the moment they walk into the center.

God demonstrated the importance of this principle and the priority He places on it decades ago. It was mid-morning on a quiet day at the Little Light House. The children were on break so no classes were in session. Only my administrative assistant and a couple of other staff members were working that day. Our workload was substantial and we had great expectations for what we hoped to get accomplished. I had just departed for a speaking engagement when an older gentleman, modestly dressed, appeared at the center. My assistant greeted the stranger who asked if she could "spare a few minutes for an old man." She smiled warmly and said, "Of course. Won't you sit down?" She then poured a cup of coffee for him and for the next hour listened to this dear man tearfully share about the loss of his wife and how much she had "loved this place called the Little Light House." A good while later, he apologized for his tears and for taking up so much of her time. Laura assured him it was no problem and expressed heartfelt appreciation to him for coming by. Before he left, he told her he'd like to come back later and "visit with Mrs. Mitchell." "But," he quickly added, "please don't mention to her that I was here or that I'm planning to return." Laura assured him she would comply with his wishes, which she did.

I had been back in the office for a few hours and had walked out to the hallway to place some mail in staff mailboxes, when

I happened to see the gentleman walk through the doors. I was struck by his kind face but there was nothing about him that seemed familiar. I greeted him, introduced myself, and asked how I could help. He asked if he could have a few minutes of my time. "Of course," I responded, and showed him to my office.

Over the next few minutes, just as he had with Laura, he sadly told me about the loss of his wife and about her attachment to the children of the Little Light House. My heart was moved with compassion as he wept over his loss. A little while later, I asked if he'd like to tour the center and he said he would. Though the children were on break at the time, he listened intently to everything I said about the children and the ways we worked with them to meet their needs.

Finally, we had made our way through the whole building. As he prepared to leave, he turned to me and said, "One more thing. I have a gift my wife wanted the Little Light House to have. Before I delivered it, though, I wanted to see if folks here would take time out of their busy schedules for an old man." He smiled warmly and then added, "And you did." With that he pulled a check for $6,000 from his pocket, made out to the Little Light House, and handed it to me. We were completely overwhelmed! Not for one minute had we imagined that this dear, plainly dressed old gentleman had the intention of blessing us the way he did.

Without a doubt, God was confirming to us we were to place a high priority on showing hospitality to strangers. Not because of what they might bring to us, but because this is simply God's will for us and for them.

Another example of an experiential lesson in the scriptural principle of hospitality came through our mail carrier. We were in our third facility, the educational wing of a church in mid-town Tulsa. Since we did not have a mailbox of our own on the property, Jay, our mail carrier, delivered our mail to our office inside. We were very grateful for his willingness to make that

Our figurative welcome mat must always be out.

extra effort and admired his faithful service. You've heard the old adage, "Neither snow nor rain nor heat nor gloom of night stays these couriers from the swift completion of their appointed rounds"?[8] Well, it could have been written just for Jay. To show our appreciation, we always had a cup of hot coffee or cold water (depending on the weather) and a doughnut for him.

His mail route responsibilities made for short visits, but soon we began to think of Jay as a very special friend. One day, as he quickly sipped his coffee, he asked if we had ever received funds from the Combined Federal Campaign. I responded that I hadn't even heard of it. He quickly explained it was a "no strings attached" program in which federal employees could direct donations to specific "approved" charities. He offered to submit our name for consideration and he did exactly that. One year later we received our first donation from the Combined Federal Campaign. Since that time (back in the eighties), we have received well over $200,000 from the Combined Federal Campaign, all because one mail carrier took the time to submit our name. We had not shown hospitality to Jay for the purpose of financial gain or, for that matter, any kind of gain. God just calls us to show hospitality. We make every effort to do so and God simply blesses.

Our commitment to "show hospitality" as Christ demands has also resulted in some unique opportunities to share the love of God with people from across the globe. Regarding the international delegations mentioned in a previous chapter, we owe a debt of gratitude to the Tulsa Global Alliance for referring delegations our way, allowing our global guests an up-close and personal look at how we minister to children with special needs and their families.

8. Inscription found on the General Post Office of New York City at 8th Avenue and 33rd Street.

When God first began bringing about such opportunities, He impressed upon our staff to study the cultures of our prospective visitors in advance. We researched what they like to eat, their customs and culture. Our staff was then coached on ways which would make these long-distance friends feel warmly welcomed. We later learned it had been reported to the Global Alliance Headquarters in Washington, the Little Light House was a favorite site. On a number of occasions, delegations told us they had been strongly encouraged by others from their nation to be sure and visit the Little Light House when they came to America. I believe with all my heart, in addition to the children's singular ability to touch the hearts of our guests, the simple practice of hospitality was largely to be credited for such positive reports. I further believe God has used the practice to bring about the major expansion of the entire Little Light House Global Impact program.

In a number of instances, our time spent with these delegations has resulted in those nations later sending international interns to study at the Little Light House for weeks or months at a time. On other occasions, relationships established through our hospitality efforts led to invitations for the Little Light House to conduct seminars and training conferences in various parts of the world. Such invitations afforded us the opportunity to provide state-of-the-art training in areas where such teaching is simply not available and, in the process, affect paradigm changes toward children with special needs across the globe. The principle of hospitality is bridge-building, to say the least. It builds bridges between countries and cultures and promotes peace and strong bonds.

It is important to note, gestures of kindness cannot be measured, and hospitality does not have to be extravagant to touch hearts. In fact, the finest example of it I ever experienced took place in a tiny village. We were in southern China visiting the families of students who were attending the school for children with special needs established by our first Chinese intern.

We had traveled a good distance to get to their village. Eventually the road conditions worsened to the extent we had to abandon our vehicle and proceed on foot. The walk was long and steep, but as we began to approach the village area, young children ran to greet us, insisting on helping us make our way up the steep incline. As we got closer, we were startled by the sound of loud fireworks. Seeing our shocked expressions, our Chinese friend assured us, "It is okay. It is the Chinese way to welcome you!" As we entered the village, men and women, young and old, stood at the doorways of barn-like, mud-brick dwellings. They were all nodding and waving as we passed.

When we reached the home of the child's family we had come to see, we were invited in. Stepping through the large opening which served as their doorway, I realized there was no electricity. As my eyes became accustomed to the darkness, I spotted a crude wooden table and some small stools in the corner of the room. There was no glass in the windows, only large square holes in the walls. There were no floors, only packed dirt. The woman of the house smiled kindly and graciously motioned for us to sit on the only seats available, leaving the family standing.

What happened next will be etched in my mind forever. She graciously offered us hot tea in little plastic Solo cups. I was struck by the sweet spirit of the family and their exemplary hospitality. Never before or since have I felt a warmer welcome from anyone, anywhere! They had only a thatched roof over their heads and no material goods whatsoever. No one in the village did. Yet the village had splurged on fireworks to welcome us, and this family, though they were very poor, still showed us Christ-like hospitality. Our remarkable Chinese friends made an indelible impression, the kind I believe God is calling us to make on everyone we meet.

Our actions must be purely motivated by our love for God and our desire to let that love flow through us and bring light to our world. When our hearts are right and we extend our hand of hospitality, God's love will shine forth to every soul who passes our way, be they stranger . . . or perhaps even an angel.

Do not neglect to show hospitality to strangers, for thereby some have entertained angels unawares.

— (Hebrews 13:2 ESV) —

Contribute to the needs of the saints and seek to show hospitality.

— (Romans 12:13 ESV) —

CHAPTER TWELVE
A WARM BLANKET
ATMOSPHERE

Love never gives up; and its faith, hope, and
patience never fail. . . . Meanwhile these three
remain: faith, hope, and love; and the greatest of
these is love.

– (1 Corinthians 13:7, 13 GNT) –

G od continued to show us additional ways as to how we could be His arms outstretched to everyone He brought our way. We were to always be prepared to share the good news of His wonderful plan of salvation with anyone who had a heart to listen. We made it our policy never to "force-feed" the gospel, but rather to be sensitive to the leadership of the Holy Spirit and to be ready to respond to the slightest prompting.

Probably one of my most treasured personal opportunities occurred one day as I was passing through the hallway on the way to my office, just after the school bells had rung signaling the start of class sessions. Though I was focused on getting to the huge stack of work on my desk, I happened to notice a pretty young mother of one of our students on her way out the door. As we passed, I saw tears in her eyes and could tell by her countenance something was very wrong. I stopped and asked her if everything was alright. She managed a slight smile and attempted to assure me she was fine, but I knew she wasn't.

A quiet voice within nudged my heart. "Joanie, would you like to talk about what's troubling you?" I asked. At first she hesitated, expressing concern about my time. I assured her there was nothing more important on my agenda that day than time spent with her.

Thankfully, she felt comfortable enough to follow me to the small conference room and, over the next hour, she felt the freedom to pour out the hurts and anguish she had experienced over the previous few months. Her brokenness stemmed from a situation involving her daughter with special needs and a church ceremony they had planned on participating in. They had spent several months in preparation and, at the last minute, those in charge had refused to allow the child to take part because of her disability. The rejection had devastated the young mother. She wept and wept as she expressed her hurt, anger, and disappointment.

We talked all morning and eventually, I was able to turn the conversation in a spiritual direction, assuring her God cared deeply for her and wanted to comfort her. I shared with her on a personal level how God had always been there for me, carrying me through the most difficult times in my life. "But Marcia, it seems like you and God are . . . well . . . like . . . best friends!" she exclaimed. "It's not that way with me."

My heart leapt with joy at this opportunity, and I quickly explained that anyone can have that kind of relationship with Christ. I went on to say how much He loves each and every one of us and is wanting to carry us through the difficult valleys of our lives. I told her how much He wanted to be there through all of her days, to guide and comfort and protect her. I shared with her that Jesus loved her so much, He even demonstrated that love for her by dying on the cross so she could have eternal life. "But Marcia," she lamented, "I'm too old and I've done too many things in my life I'm ashamed of!"

I had to chuckle. She couldn't have been more than thirty. "First of all, you are never too old to accept God's love and plan of salvation for your life. And second, Jesus took care of all of our sins when He suffered and died. He took the punishment we deserve." Her face was filled with doubt.

At that moment an old Baptist hymn came to mind. I was quiet for a moment and then spoke. "Joanie, have you ever heard the old hymn about being washed whiter than snow?" Her eyes widened as she said, "No, I haven't." I smiled and said, "Oh my! I have such wonderful news for you!"

I shared just a few lines from the hymn I had sung since I was a young child.

> *What can wash away my sins?*
> *Nothing but the blood of Jesus.*
> *What can make me whole again?*
> *Nothing but the blood of Jesus.*
> *Oh precious is the flow*
> *That makes me white as snow;*
> *No other fount I know,*
> *Nothing but the blood of Jesus.*[9]

She was amazed as I explained further all that Christ had done for us. A while later, when I asked if she would like to surrender her life to Christ, she beamed and nodded. So, we slipped into the little chapel around the corner from my office and I was able to unfold the whole wonderful gospel message of salvation. I told my sweet new friend how she could be "best friends with God," as she had put it. We prayed and that very day, this precious young mom entered into a personal relationship with Jesus Christ. I'll never forget the look on her beautiful face when we said the final

---

9. Robert Lowry, "Nothing but the Blood of Jesus," (1876).

"Amen." When I opened my eyes, her face was radiant! All the worry, the pain, and the grief had completely disappeared. She was glowing. She couldn't wait to tell anyone and everyone who would listen about her decision and her Savior. She told staff members who happened to be right outside the door and then as she went out to lunch with some friends, she kept on telling anyone who would listen.

A couple of hours later, this excited young mom called to thank me again for the time we had shared. She expressed her gratitude over and over, and kept saying she felt like a butterfly, as though she had been in a cocoon and had finally been set free. I loved hearing that and with such joy in my heart I responded, "Oh, Joanie, you are free! Christ has set you free and no matter what you may go through, He will always be there for you . . . closer than your very breath!"

When I returned to my desk, the stacks of paperwork were still there. I smiled. There would always be a pile of desk work, but moments like those with Joanie didn't come about every day. My heart overflowed with gratitude to the Lord for allowing me to be in the right place at the right time to minister to her aching heart. There was no question He would continue to orchestrate moments like this for each of us as staff members, as long as we remain sensitive to His leadership.

Another classic story of one of those golden opportunities occurred in the nineties, not long after we had moved into our new facility. A young woman called, expressing interest in our volunteer program. Diane had heard we sometimes allowed children of volunteers to serve as typical peer models in our classrooms. She loved the idea of working with children with special needs, and the thought of having her own child under the same roof with her was icing on the cake. She had heard great reports about the Little Light House, and that the center offered quality, state-of-the-art, individualized services.

There was only one drawback from her perspective. Diane had also heard we were a Christian center. In her words, "I just didn't know about getting involved with a bunch of Bible thumpers and Jesus freaks." But her desire to work with children with special needs won out. She came, she interviewed, and both she and her child were accepted into our volunteer program. She began her volunteer service and seemed to be enjoying it.

One day, the opportunity was provided for children in one of the classrooms to ask Jesus into their hearts. One little boy had made that decision and was so excited about it, the teacher in that classroom allowed him to announce his wonderful news on the intercom which was heard throughout the center. Diane heard the child squeal with glee as his little voice came through each classroom speaker: "I just asked Jesus into my heart!" Visibly disturbed, she turned to the teacher in the class she was serving in and asked, "They're not going to . . . do that to my child, are they? I mean . . . I don't want her brainwashed or anything." The teacher smiled and gently responded assuringly. "Don't worry. She'll hear about Jesus but nothing will be forced on her. It will be okay." Something about the soothing tone of the teacher and her kind manner seemed to satisfy Diane.

She continued to volunteer and seemed to grow more comfortable with every passing day. Then a few months later she happened to be attending a self-improvement seminar in Oklahoma City. One of the speakers was a priest who began to talk in general about the love of God. She approached him at the break. "I don't know about this love of God stuff," she said, "but as you were talking, it made me think about this place in Tulsa where I volunteer. Every time you walk in the door of that place, it feels like a soft warm blanket is being wrapped around you." The priest's face lit up. "That's the love of God you are feeling! Tell me more about this place. I'd like to visit there."

It is God's love flowing through us that will draw the lost to want to seek Him.

A couple of weeks later, Diane met the priest at the Little Light House for a tour. Afterward, I invited them to my office for coffee. As I visited with this man of God about the miracles which had led up to the founding of the Little Light House and the miraculous way God had continued to work, Diane seemed to be drinking in our conversation.

It wasn't long after, she asked the teacher in the classroom in which she volunteered if she could answer some questions for her regarding what it meant to be "saved." The teacher smiled warmly and later that day they stole away to the little chapel down the hall.

There, in that tiny room, another soul was ushered into the kingdom of God. Again, as with the young mom, an amazing transformation took place. Our volunteer who had been so concerned about working in a Christian setting changed before our very eyes. She couldn't wait to begin professing her new faith to everyone. In fact, the day she asked Jesus into her heart, she went home and led her husband to the Lord. A month later, they accepted an invitation to attend one of our Board of Directors meetings where they spoke about their life-changing decision to follow Christ.

I believe both of these stories and countless others began with our staff generating a warm blanket atmosphere of love. For it is God's love flowing through us that will draw the lost to want to seek Him. When they do, we, as ambassadors for Christ, must be ready to present the great news of salvation through Christ.

No matter where we are or what we are doing in life, we all have a mission field filled with precious souls who are searching for a way to fill the hole in their heart that only our Lord Jesus Christ can fill. As Christians, we are called to abide in Christ and remain sensitive to the leadership of the Holy Spirit so that when one of those souls crosses our path, we might be the arms of Christ ready to usher them into His marvelous kingdom.

Beloved, let us love one another, for love is from God, and whoever loves has been born of God and knows God. Anyone who does not love does not know God, because God is love. In this the love of God was made manifest among us, that God sent his only Son into the world, so that we might live through him.

– (1 John 4:7-9 ESV) –

CHAPTER THIRTEEN

DIVINE CONNECTIONS

*Do not be anxious about anything, but in
everything by prayer and supplication with
thanksgiving let your requests be made known to
God. And the peace of God, which surpasses all
understanding, will guard your hearts and your
minds in Christ Jesus.*

– (Philippians 4:6-7 ESV) –

Prayer has always been man's way of communing with
God. It is through prayer we petition our loving Father for
strength for the day, wisdom for our decisions, and help in
times of trouble. The entire history of the Little Light House is
a living testimony to God's desire to respond to such prayers by
pouring out His goodness upon us. God's provision and answers
to prayer have come to us in many forms and have addressed
needs both minute and monumental.

At speaking engagements, I've often been asked to share
favorite stories from my book, *Milestones & Miracles*, which reflect
such demonstrations of God's love and blessing. One such story,

and a favorite of many, occurred during a time when finances were so tight the decision was regretfully made to eliminate donuts from our budget. A donut and a hot cup of coffee had always been our way of thanking our volunteers for their time, but we no longer could afford the sugary treats for them. I knew if we wanted donuts we would have to look to a heavenly source to provide them. A week later a man we had never met contacted us by phone. He said he had a real desire to help the Little Light House and wished he could make a large donation but didn't have the means to do so. However, he explained, he did have a donut shop and wondered if we could use donuts. He said he would like to contribute as many as we could use. As amazing as it seems, he donated ninety dozen donuts that week and continued contributing the delightful confections for the next decade.

On another occasion, a civic club was lined up to move the Little Light House from the third floor of an educational wing of a church to a one-story educational complex of another church approximately five miles away. With inclement weather predicted, prayers were lifted up for a safe and successful move. It was a frigid day but the move went perfectly. As the last piece of furniture was carried into the new facility, the sky opened up with an onslaught of sleet. Later we learned that it had actually been sleeting across the entire city for hours, except for one small section: the section between our old and our new facility. One worker later commented it was as though God held a huge umbrella over that area the entire time they were working. Those civic club members are still telling this story today.

I also recall the time when an increasing number of medically fragile children were making their way to the Little Light House. Consequently, the need to have a registered nurse on staff became critical. Our limited funding, however, only allowed for the replacement of a teaching assistant who had moved away. I reasoned with the Lord about how serious our situation was and waited for Him to reveal what we should do. Soon after, a young woman walked through the door and asked if she might apply for the teaching assistant position. During the interview, when asked about her credentials, she somewhat apologetically explained that her background was actually in nursing. "But," she continued, "I believe I have a calling to work with children with visual impairments. That's where my heart is, and I felt God leading me here." I was able to hire her in a dual capacity as teaching assistant and nurse. Sherry was the first of a number of nurses who have served our students since that time.

Another unforgettable day, the Little Light House supply of tissues, paper towels, and toilet paper became utterly depleted. The need had become desperate, but because of the increased costs related to an expansion of our facility, funds were not available for replenishing the stock. All we could do was pray. Then, inexplicably, out of the blue, a large Kimberly Clark truck pulled into the Little Light House loading dock and unloaded more donated paper products than our storage could even hold!

God is able to meet all needs from the most minute to the most monumental.

There was also the pivotal time in our history when, burdened by an ever-growing waiting list, the Little Light House leaders felt led of God to begin looking into expansion options. They decided the ideal scenario would be to enlarge existing facilities at 36th & Yale. The Little Light House, however, had no more land on which to expand. Though it seemed like a long shot, it was decided to approach the church which owned the land next to our school property. We knew it would take a miracle to acquire that land, as the church had been on that corner adjacent to us long before we built. We prayerfully set a date for our representatives to meet with church representatives. During that meeting the pastor expressed amazement over the timing of our inquiry, explaining that the very night before, the church leadership had met to discuss the future of the church and the possibility of moving to another location. It was only a short while later we learned the church was indeed willing to sell their property. Over the next year, God confirmed we were to buy it as He worked through precious souls in the community to provide the $1,000,000 needed for the acquisition of the land.

Each and every one of these narratives is true, and there are literally hundreds if not thousands more which have taken place throughout Little Light House history. I could easily fill the pages of this book with these stories alone. The accounts are varied in nature but in each situation, believers relied on a divine connection to our Heavenly Father, and it was by His mighty power responding to our prayers these miracles unfolded.

Prayer is critical to the success of any ministry. Nothing overshadows it and nothing can replace it. Prayer is our link to our Heavenly Father. It is through our communication with Him that we gain our strength, our direction, our hope, and provision. He is our source and without Him we can do nothing. Adrian Rogers said it best: "There is no promise God cannot keep, no prayer God cannot answer, and no problem too hard for Him to solve."[10] In short, we simply cannot do God's work, God's way without seeking God's guidance. For it is only as we maintain our divine connection with Him that our work will be to His glory. Of this we can be certain!

> *. . . praying at all times in the Spirit, with all prayer and supplication. To that end keep alert with all perseverance, making supplication for all the saints . . .*
> – (Ephesians 6:18 ESV) –

---

10. Adrian Rogers, *Adrianisms: The Wit and Wisdom of Adrian Rogers* (Memphis, TN: Love Worth Finding Ministries, 2015), 16.

CHAPTER FOURTEEN

ONE IN THE SPIRIT

*I therefore, a prisoner for the Lord, urge you to
walk in a manner worthy of the calling to which
you have been called, with all humility and
gentleness, with patience, bearing with one another
in love, eager to maintain the unity of the Spirit in
the bond of peace.*

– (Ephesians 4:1-3 ESV) –

One of the greatest factors which can destroy the
effectiveness of any ministry or organization is a sense
of division. Without a sense of unity, people tend to
pull in opposite directions, communication breaks down, and
energy is wasted on irrelevant issues which shouldn't even be a
concern. There are any number of matters that can creep into the
workplace causing contention and strife. Innocent by-standers
are often caught in the wake of dissension and discord.

Because the Little Light House is a Christian center,
oftentimes new staff members come to us expecting a sort of
utopia. When I used to conduct the interviews, I always made

sure applicants fully understood, as a Little Light House staff, though dedicated to following the Lord, we are all human, just like every other ministry or business. There will be differences of opinion, work styles, and ways of doing things. Therefore, in order to preserve unity, Little Light House management stresses to the staff the importance of maintaining and nurturing good working relationships and even provides coaching on how to do that (see chapter 15 called "A Matter of the Heart"). But likely the most important and valuable practice which contributes to a positive sense of peace is something which has long been known as "Flock."

Flock has been the way we have started our days since we first opened the doors of the Little Light House in 1972. On that very first morning, though we were few in number, our volunteers and myself and our first teacher gathered for a time of devotions and prayer before the children arrived. Our young teacher called that time "Flock" and it has been "Flock" ever since. We maintain the practice to this day. It only lasts twenty minutes but that short time together sets the tone for the whole day. Hearts are joined together. Burdens are sometimes shared. Answers to prayer are celebrated and the needs of the ministry are lifted up to the Lord. It is also our way of putting God first as we give Him the first part of our day.

Little Light House Flock time provides spiritual nourishment to our staff. Due to our class schedule for the children, four days a week, our Flock time must be quite brief, lasting less than half an hour. But because Fridays are a professional work day for the staff, a one-hour Bible study is conducted on that day. Special speakers are brought in on occasion, but always the focus is on drawing nearer to the heart of our Heavenly Father.

Of course, individual staff members themselves must be abiding in Christ. They each must be engaged in drawing near to Him on a daily basis and have a heart's desire to be led by the Holy Spirit. Each is responsible for keeping their own heart in a pursuit of holiness. Corporate prayer and devotional time tend to nurture that inner desire to abide in Christ. It also encourages open and transparent communication between staff members as well as with God. It promotes a spirit of love and patience with one another. It teaches and reminds each one present how God has instructed us to live. It also renews God's purpose and vision in the hearts of all and it keeps Christ as the cornerstone and focus of our hearts individually and corporately.

> *Corporate prayer and devotional time tend to nurture that inner desire to abide in Christ.*

There was only one time in our history when our staff did not all come together each morning for Flock. It was a painful period but one which taught me a great deal about how to maintain a spirit of unity and harmony with a staff representing multiple denominations. I believe that lesson bears sharing.

I recall we were all concerned about the health of a particular child. As we were praying for him one morning, the tone of the prayer began to take on the feel of a theological debate. Voices were rising in intensity and there was tension in the air. It was obvious some had different theological views about healing than others, and each camp was set on convincing the other their way was right. I could see the threat of division.

I sought the Lord in prayer and He impressed upon my heart to instruct the staff to pair up with someone with whom they were comfortable praying. Each set of two was to pray together each morning until I instructed otherwise. We prayed in pairs for more than a month as I sought the Lord about how to handle this difficult and highly sensitive situation. Meanwhile I heard from both factions that if I didn't concur with their approach to prayer and their theology, they would have to resign. I knew they were each sincere, but I also knew their differences were causing an unhealthy divisiveness. I was at a loss as to what to do. Finally, almost a month later, it was as though a fog lifted as God led me to this Scripture.

> *Flee the evil desires of youth and pursue righteous-*
> *ness, faith, love and peace, along with those who call*
> *on the Lord out of a pure heart. Don't have anything*
> *to do with foolish and stupid arguments, because you*
> *know they produce quarrels. And the Lord's servant*
> *must not be quarrelsome but must be kind to every-*
> *one, able to teach, not resentful. Opponents must*
> *be gently instructed, in the hope that God will grant*
> *them repentance leading them to a knowledge of the*
> *truth, and that they will come to their senses and*
> *escape from the trap of the devil, who has taken them*
> *captive to do his will (2 Timothy 2:22–26 NIV).*

God began to reveal to me the Little Light House was to be a ministry that bridged the gap between differing theologies. All that really mattered was that we were all believers and devoted followers of Christ and each of us had a personal relationship with Him. How staff members prayed was up to them, but I was to tell the staff that at the Little Light House, there would be no arguments, no quarreling, and no theological debates, before, during, or after our prayer time together. God wanted to hear from pure hearts which had enough love and respect for one another to allow each to embrace their own theological beliefs. Therefore, in a spirit of love, when we prayed corporately, our prayers were to be prayed in a manner that would not stir up division and in a way that would demonstrate love and respect for each and every staff member. How individuals prayed within their own hearts was up to them. But surely it would please our Father God most to hear our prayers expressed in one accord.

Sadly, two staff members resigned as a result of the new Flock policy, and certainly that grieved my heart. However, a sweetness of spirit returned within our staff and never again did I have to suspend Flock.

After this experience, I drafted a set of Flock Guidelines focused on preserving mutual respect and solidarity within a staff representing such a wide range of denominations and theological perspectives. We continue to seek ways to hone and monitor those guidelines to ensure they remain an effective tool. In addition, in the interviewing process, candidates are made aware that any discussion of controversial issues such as political views are to be avoided.

There are so many benefits to this time together it is hard to recount them all. During these very special times of fellowship, the focus is placed on the real reason for the Little Light House and how we can most effectively bring glory to God through our work. Our Flock times often include testimonies which lead to greater understanding between staff members. Sometimes, it is an opportunity for cleansing and restoration of relationships. It is also a time for praising our Heavenly Father, focusing on who He is and all He has done for us.

Always the needs of our staff and the center are prayed over. Prayers are lifted up on behalf of children, volunteers, board members, and even constituents who have expressed needs. For most staff members, it is the most important part of their day. It is their time to get centered—Christ-centered—and it affects everything that happens the rest of the day.

Prayer is vital to a spirit of oneness in Christ. Whether you are applying this principle to a family, a ministry, or a church, being one in the Spirit is essential if we want to be used of God.

> *So if there is any encouragement in Christ, any comfort from love, any participation in the Spirit, any affection and sympathy, complete my joy by being of the same mind, having the same love, being in full accord and of one mind. Do nothing from selfish ambition or conceit, but in humility count others more significant than yourselves.*
>
> – (Philippians 2:1-3 ESV) –

CHAPTER FIFTEEN
A MATTER OF THE HEART

If your brother sins, go and show him his fault in
private; if he listens to you,
you have won your brother.

– (Matthew 18:15 NASB) –

Marriages split over it. Friendships dissolve because of it. Families spend years apart from each other and sometimes never reconcile because of it. Valuable employees walk off the job in the midst of it and in its aftermath, business partners go their separate ways, giving up dreams and aspirations they once shared. It is so destructive, even countries go to war because of it. Most assuredly, it has the power to completely extinguish the bright light of ministries and works of God.

It's been around since Adam and Eve and continues to wreak havoc to this day. Its agenda is to create division, misery, and ruin. We've all experienced it to one degree or another. For some, it has resulted in such personal devastation that they never recover from it. So what is this dynamic force which leaves such an enormous path of destruction behind? Very simply put, it is conflict in relationships.

God is well aware of this threat and addresses this issue throughout the Old and New Testament. Over and over, He makes it clear: He is all about relationships. He demonstrates this through the trinity of the Father, the Son, and the Holy Spirit. We are made in His image and therefore we are made to be in right relationship with Him and with others. He even goes so far as to say we can't be at odds with our sisters and brothers in Christ and truly love God. 1 John 4:20 (NET) tells us, "*If anyone says 'I love God' and yet hates his fellow Christian, he is a liar, because the one who does not love his fellow Christian whom he has seen cannot love God whom he has not seen.*"

We are to take care of relationships. This is God's mandate to us.

We are to take care of our relationships. This is God's mandate to us. Whether on the job, at home, relating to our neighbors, in our church family, or in our circle of friends, we're to place high value on and be committed to preserving relationships. In fact, God's Word goes so far as to say this is one of the two most important commandments: "'*And you shall love the Lord your God with all your heart and with all your soul, and with all your mind, and with all your strength.' The second is this, 'You shall love your neighbor as yourself.' There is no other commandment greater than these*" (Mark 12:30–31 NASB). To do the work of God in a way that honors Him, we must understand and embrace this vitally important principle.

Problems arise in relationships because we are all different. We have different tastes, different backgrounds, and different preferences. We are each wired differently, responding emotionally in different ways to different circumstances. We all walk into relationships hiding past experiences which have affected our attitudes, fears, expectations, and behaviors. In addition, we all have different temperaments, different love languages, and different gifts. Some of us, by nature, are intense and sensitive. Others are laid-back and rarely take offense. Some are goal-setters and self-starters and some are not. When we all get thrown into life together, conflicts are bound to arise.

So what do we do when those conflicts raise their ugly heads and begin to taunt us? How are we to react? What are we to do? Scripture makes it plain. First, we are to respond with humility, sensitivity, and kindness, with every effort to bring about harmony in the relationship. We are to pray blessings for those with whom we are in conflict. *"To sum up, all of you be harmonious, sympathetic, brotherly, kindhearted, and humble in spirit; not returning evil for evil or insult for insult, but giving a blessing instead; for you were called for the very purpose that you might inherit a blessing. For, the one who desires life, to love and see good days, must keep his tongue from evil and His lips from speaking deceit"* (1 Peter 3:8–11 NASB).

God's Word also tells us we are to make sure we have asked God to give us a genuine love for the other person. In such circumstances, it is vital that we examine our own hearts, and identify any fault of our own which might be at play in the situation. We must be sure that our hearts are right and our feelings are not based on selfishness, jealousy, or any other wrong motive. If we can't say that is true, then we must ask God to help us lay aside our selfish desires and pride and instead, value the other person's feelings and thoughts even above our own. Last but not least, we need to ask ourselves if we have a forgiving spirit toward the source of our conflict. Of course, none of this can be done in our own strength. We must constantly rely on the Lord.

Still, try as we might, situations will arise when we, as humans, end up in relationship conflicts. If we find there is tension and stress in the relationship, Scripture teaches us we are to go directly to that person (or persons) privately and sensitively and attempt to work out our differences.

Over the years, I have seen this principle work time after time, both on a personal level and in the lives of my staff and board. It has been my observation that when hearts are right and this principle is applied, relationships are restored and typically strengthened.

The state of the heart is the key to this principle. When considering approaching another individual about a relationship conflict, time should be spent in prayer asking God to purify our own motives and reveal any fault that may have been hidden from our view.

Our motive in approaching the source of conflict must be to save or restore the relationship. Ideally that needs to be communicated up front. It simply won't work if the intent is to go for any other purpose. If we go to vent or cast blame, this will only exacerbate the situation. Both parties must be able to acknowledge their own part in creating the conflict. Just as it takes two surfaces rubbing together to create friction, so it is in relationships. Therefore, resolution calls for genuine transparency and humility. It helps immensely to first verbally acknowledge one's own flaws to the other person and acknowledge any personal responsibility for creating the conflict. Typically, when one party can see that the other is willing to acknowledge their part in the decline in the relationship, they are more likely to feel free to acknowledge their own part in the problem.

It may take time to work through the factors which have been contributing to the problems. It's imperative to keep remembering that the desired outcome is to understand each other better and to strengthen the relationship. That ultimate goal needs to be communicated early on.

The process is as important as the outcome. In some isolated cases, even when the heart is pure and the intent is to restore or preserve the relationship, two people or parties may reach an impasse. At this point, it is scriptural and in order for the two experiencing the conflict to go to a person next in line in authority to appeal for help in reaching a resolution.

Many find obeying this Biblical principle extremely challenging. I can recall many times in the past when staff members came to me, complaining about something another staff member was doing which had become a source of annoyance or which they felt was wrong or represented the ministry poorly.

Having been exposed to this scriptural principle years ago, I would typically pose the following question to the one airing the complaint. "What did this staff member say to you when you spoke with them about your concerns?" Typically, they had never mentioned the issue to the staff member with whom they were frustrated. Oftentimes, my encouragement to go directly to the source was met with great resistance, especially if it was a subordinate complaining about a supervisor. But, time and again, when the principle was applied, I saw positive outcomes.

Probably the best part of this principle is that it allows us to see our own faults and gives us a chance to correct them. If several different people come to us at different times with the same observation, chances are we've got an area of our life we need to work on. It's a principle not applied much in our society, but it is a powerful Biblical principle; and I can say from personal experiences and observation, God's approach to conflict resolution simply works. It preserves and restores relationships and molds character in those applying it. Ultimately, it is pleasing in the sight of God.

Conflict in relationships creates strife. Strife creates division. Division destroys unity and harmony, and without unity and harmony, we cannot have a positive witness for Christ. Therefore, if we want to be effective in furthering the kingdom of God and leading our world to Christ, we as Christians must be diligent in preserving and protecting our relationships. It is, plain and simple, a matter of the heart and keeping the state of our heart right with God and man.

*Be kind to one another, tender-hearted, forgiving
each other, just as God in Christ also has
forgiven you.*

– (Ephesians 4:32 NASB) –

*Since you have in obedience to the truth purified
your souls for a sincere love of the brethren,
fervently love one another from the heart . . .*

– (1 Peter 1:22 NASB) –

CHAPTER SIXTEEN

A HIGHER CALLING

*Only conduct yourselves in a manner worthy of
the gospel of Christ, so that whether I come and see
you or remain absent, I will hear of you that you
are standing firmly in one spirit, with one mind
striving together for the faith of the gospel.*

– (Philippian 1:27 NASB) –

Several decades ago God began speaking clearly to my heart about still another element which can compromise the effectiveness of any work operating in the name of Christ. It is one which requires a difficult stand for the leadership of any ministry, but it is vitally important if a work for God is going to bring glory to His name. God began revealing this scriptural mandate to me when the Little Light House was still in its formative years.

I had been pondering for some time whether we as a Christian center could legitimately place Christian lifestyle expectations on our staff outside of working hours. I also wondered if we should have the same expectations for the members of our Board of

Directors. I knew, as a Christian center, our staff, board members, and I were subject to close scrutiny by the families we served as well as the community. Our actions at work and outside of work projected either a positive or a negative witness for Christ. After months of seeking divine direction, God used one particular incident to make His answer crystal clear to me.

It all began one afternoon as I listened to several young staff members excitedly talking about getting together that evening to celebrate the birthday of one of our teachers. I didn't know the details of their conversation, only that they were planning on going to a movie. The next day there was a lot of giggling while they ate their lunch as they talked about their evening the night before. I was glad they had such a good time but was distressed to learn the movie they had gone to had been R-rated due to sexual content. Though I felt a strong check in my spirit and a knot in my stomach, I didn't feel I was to say anything to them at the time. After all, it was done on their own time and it was outside working hours.

I wrestled and prayed about the whole matter that night and in the days to come, seeking the Lord about whether I could or should say anything about the matter. As the days passed, my mind wrestled with the issue. Working at the Little Light House was a form of employment. The staff members came to work and they got paid. But, I reasoned, we were also a Christian center and a ministry and as such we were committed to keeping Jesus as our cornerstone. When the Little Light House had taken a stand as a Christian developmental center, I felt we assumed a new level of responsibility to maintain a positive witness both corporately and individually. A running debate continued on in my mind as I prayed for God to show me His will in the matter.

A week later I ran into a dear friend who happened to be in a Bible study group with one of our therapists. We chatted briefly and she mentioned how much she thought of the Little Light House staff member and how greatly she enjoyed being in the Bible study with her. She then went on to say how much they had missed her at the Bible study the week before (the same night as the birthday get-together which had taken place at the R-rated movie). Her next words were the ones that pierced my heart. "I understand she was at a Little Light House function that night," my friend continued.

I'm sure I looked stunned and for certain I was speechless. That's when it occurred to me. She was hardly at a "Little Light House function"! Nonetheless, that was the perception. My face flushed as I thought about the possibility of a parent, volunteer, or constituent seeing this group of Little Light House staff members all entering this questionable movie together.

I went home that day feeling distraught about the whole situation. As I sought God's leading through His Word, He confirmed my concerns as I read in 1 John 2:15–16 (ESV): "*Do not love the world or the things in the world. If anyone loves the world, the love of the Father is not in him. For all that is in the world—the desires of the flesh and the desires of the eyes and pride in possessions—is not from the Father but is from the world.*"

As I read these words, I knew. When we become Christians and profess our faith to our world, we are called to be a light, a reflection of God's goodness, gospel, and love. How can we be a light if we are blending in with the world?

"But Lord," I prayed, "can we expect a higher standard of our workers than the rest of the world would expect?" They are employees. Yet, my heart resisted, they are also ministry representatives. It was then God brought to mind Ephesians 5:8 (NLT): "*For once you were full of darkness, but now you have light from the Lord. So live as people of light!*" In order for the light of the Little Light House to shine brightly, our world must see us as people of light. I saw clearly this was essential to our mission.

I continued to seek God throughout the weekend. The following Monday, in the morning devotional time when all of our staff met together, I told them I had something on my heart I needed to share with them. I described my struggle and my seeking the Lord in the matter of staff conduct outside of work hours. I assured them I knew they had never intended any harm, but as transparently as I knew how, I told them about my visit with the friend of one of our staff members. Last but not least, I revealed the perception the friend had: that the staff outing had been a Little Light House function. I explained how others, seeing them enter the movie together, could have had the same impression.

As a group, we then spent time reflecting on the truth of Ephesians 5:8 and the witness we each have in and outside of the Little Light House. After a time of introspection and reflection on God's higher calling on our lives, the hearts of the whole staff came into agreement. They recognized, though they had intended no harm, their actions could have compromised our witness. We were all united in the realization, as representatives of Christ and the Little Light House ministry, we must be constantly aware of our actions. We must be diligent to live in a way that honors our Lord, inside and outside of our working hours.

Within the last decade, with the nation experiencing serious moral decay, Little Light House leadership took a deeper look at this issue. It seemed there was increasing confusion and misconception about exactly what the Bible says about standards of conduct for Christians. Many hours of prayer and Bible study were devoted to identifying exactly what those standards are according to the Word of God. We didn't want to become legalistic, yet we did feel it vitally important to draw clear Biblical lines in the sand and make certain all of those involved with our ministry understood what the Bible says about how we are to live our lives.

Board and staff members came into agreement and a code of Biblical standards of conduct was drafted, as well as a commitment form to these standards. To commit to such scriptural standards is a high calling indeed, but it is without question a part of ministry and essential to having a positive witness to the gospel of Christ.

With all of this said, it is important to note the part grace must also play in any ministry. God imparted this understanding in our hearts a number of years ago when one of our young staff members asked to meet with myself and our associate director. When she entered my office, her eyes were bloodshot from crying. When we asked what was on her heart, she was unable to speak at first. Rather, she just wept. When she was finally able to find her voice, she began to share through her tears how she had become involved with a young man and made a terrible mistake. She knew what she had done was wrong but now it was too late. She was pregnant and had been left alone by him to deal with the challenges awaiting her. She tearfully asked for our forgiveness. She expressed she had been sincere when she signed our 24/7 lifestyle code of conduct commitment form reflecting her understanding of the higher calling for Little Light House staff members. She felt terrible about her indiscretion and expressed a willingness to resign. We told her she was of course forgiven and we wanted to pray about the whole situation. We did.

Christian ministries must realize the importance of their role in shining light into a dark world.

Of course, our concern was the witness and how God could be most glorified in the midst of these circumstances. We took the matter to our management team which is made up of the heads of each department of the Little Light House. When we did, they prayerfully considered the matter and came to the following conclusion. None of us are without sin. God calls us to repent of our sins and this young woman had. It was decided to invite her to remain on staff, but she was asked to share openly and transparently with our staff, asking their forgiveness as well. She quickly agreed to talk to them the next morning.

The next day, when we were all gathered for our morning devotional and prayer time, she was given a chance to speak.

As she sadly related to the staff all that she had shared with my associate director and myself, the staff listened with compassion and sensitive hearts. She told them about her pregnancy and that the young man was no longer in the picture. She then asked if they could forgive her for compromising the witness of the Little Light House. One staff member then softly asked, "What about the baby?" The young woman bravely spoke up and with great conviction she said, "I'm going to have the baby and keep it."

I'll never forget what happened next. The entire staff burst into applause. There was a beautiful spirit of forgiveness in the room that morning as our staff loved on this one among us who had bared her heart. One of us was hurting and therefore the whole body of Christ was hurting with her. No one sat in judgment. Each heart was filled with love.

The young woman also wrote a letter to the parents of the Little Light House children. She apologized for not representing the Lord and the Little Light House in a positive way through her actions, and told how she had received love and forgiveness from the Little Light House staff and leadership. The families also responded with love. Months later, her beautiful baby was welcomed into the world and became a beloved part of the Little Light House family. It has been said, "Within the body of Christ, we're not perfect, we're just forgiven." How true. We need each other. We need to function as one, caring about each other passionately. We are to hurt when others hurt, rejoice when others rejoice, and always treat others as we would want to be treated. In so doing, we let the light of God's love shine through us.

There are some who might view this as a radical stand and many might question whether or not it is valid to expect a commitment to Biblical standards of conduct at all times from their ministry board and staff. The fact of the matter is, however, that each of us as Christians is called to those very standards whether we are representing a ministry or not. We are all representing our Lord Jesus Christ and we are to be reflections of Him, no matter where we are or what we are doing. When representing a Christian ministry, that responsibility is heightened. People look to ministry members to exemplify the Christian life.

Of course, there are no perfect people, in or out of ministry settings. But it is important that Christian ministries or any Christian entity realize their corporate responsibility to be committed to shining a light in a dark world. When a Christian shows disregard for Scripture and willingly and knowingly gives in to a life that is contrary to the Word of God, their witness is bound to have a negative impact on those around them. When representing a Christian entity, that negative impact is magnified. That is why we have an even greater responsibility to reflect Christ in every aspect of our lives. Are we perfect? No. Are we forgiven and committed to a positive witness? We absolutely must be!

As Christians, we are called to be a light to our world, and to do that we must recognize our higher calling. It is a calling to reflect a Biblical code of conduct in all we say and do. Right along with that comes the need to respond to each other with love and grace. As we do so, the light of God's love shining through us will draw our world toward our loving, forgiving Heavenly Father, and therein lies the ultimate mission of any ministry.

Do your best to present yourself to God as one
approved, a worker who has no need to be
ashamed, rightly handling the word of truth.

– (2 Timothy 2:15 ESV) –

CHAPTER SEVENTEEN

ALL HANDS ON DECK

*Just as our bodies have many parts and each part
has a special function, so it is with Christ's body.
We are many parts of one body, and we all
belong to each other. In his grace, God has given us
different gifts for doing certain things well.*

– (Romans 12:4-6 NLT) –

A cheerful voice comes over the intercom: "All hands on deck. All hands on deck." These are words which have echoed through the halls of the Little Light House for decades; in fact, since the very beginning of the ministry. The announcement is then typically followed with instructions regarding where everyone is to report and within minutes, you will see all available teachers, secretaries, therapists, and yes, even the executive director file out of their offices and gather joyfully in a designated spot to accomplish a task. It might be unloading a truck of donated supplies, setting up chairs and tables for a donor banquet or preparing for a professional conference or student graduation. The tasks are varied, but everyone on staff pitches in to get the job done in short order.

Following each event at the center, you'll see the same thing: everyone pitching in and lending a hand. "Many hands make light work," we like to say. Every time I hear someone light-heartedly make that statement, I think to myself, that phrase has a double meaning. It not only makes the work less burdensome, it also makes the light of God shine through and "work" effectively!

The all-hands-on-deck approach is as much a part of the Little Light House DNA as beginning each day with prayer. Of course, without question, everyone has their role and each staff member is there to fulfill their particular function within the body of Christ. We believe that's how God intended it. However, we also believe God calls us to work as a team, as the body of Christ, and exhorts us not to consider ourselves better than each other.

Even the Little Light House approach to special education reflects God's plan for His people to function as "one body in Christ." It is a Biblical principle which works on a very practical level. The application of this principle involves physical therapists, occupational therapists, our low vision specialist, school nurse and our assistive technology specialists, working hand-in-hand with our teachers and associates. Together they set goals, assess each child's progress and plan activities designed to

> *Each member of the body must see themselves as a part of the whole, not as an island.*

help each child develop to his or her maximum potential. No single professional is considered superior to another. Each area of expertise is vital to each child's development. The therapists know how crucial the teachers' contribution is. The teachers and their associates greatly value the therapists. The entire children's services team is fully aware and sensitive to the fact they couldn't be there without the efforts of the administrative team. With the staff as a whole working together, the children receive far greater benefits than they would otherwise.

The wisdom found in Romans 12:4 is an indispensable principle for any ministry. Each member of the body must see themselves as a part of the whole, not as an island. This leaves no room for professional pride or professionals being territorial. Such attitudes result in divisiveness and without question, it is most assuredly a poor witness. I would liken it to an orchestra in concert. If one member of the orchestra deliberately tries to play his instrument louder than all the others when the music doesn't call for it, or another musician simply refuses to play his part, the symphony is compromised. We must all follow the lead of our divine conductor, and use our individual gifts for the purpose of fulfilling our unique role in the body of believers.

At the Little Light House, one of our major fund-raising events is called Mini-Laps. If you ask most staff members, they'll tell you it is their favorite. The parents appeal for sponsorships for their individual children. Then, on Mini-Laps day, the children all come in costumes according to the theme. During the event, they make their way around a little mini-track one at a time to the sound of themed music and the cheers of hundreds of spectators. Their milestones are celebrated as each one rounds the tiny track in whatever manner they are able. One year they might complete their short lap in a wagon turned into a beautiful float. The next year, they may take their turn using a walker their parents have decorated. It is the highlight of the year and the staff pours heart and soul into the event, using all their gifts and talents.

I am always amazed at the extraordinary decorations and the superb organization of this unique celebration. Charming chalk drawings sketched by talented staff members adorn the sidewalks welcoming the families and friends. The mini-track is always transformed into a set depending upon the chosen motif. I have the joy of being one of the emcees for the event and scripts are always ready for us, with carefully prepared information to share about each child's victories and milestones. As I think about that remarkable gathering, I am reminded of all the talents which are represented to produce a successful Mini-Laps.

The development team must work hard to promote it and equip the parents to obtain sponsorships. They also arrange for sound technicians and handle all the decorations for the event. The administrative team makes certain the grounds look great and address a myriad of other details. The children's services staff members prepare the scripts for the emcees and practice with the children. So much more goes into the event, but it all comes together because the entire staff is functioning as one body. If one part of that body fails to function, it affects all the others. One year, the main coordinator of the event had an unavoidable emergency. The rest of the staff pitched in and did more than their part, resulting in a beautiful event which ran seamlessly. They did so gladly, because that is just how the body of Christ works.

Operating as one body in Christ is essential for any ministry or work of the Lord. It is only by applying this vital principle that genuine teamwork is achieved, and it is only through teamwork our shared goals can be realized.

Now you are the body of Christ, and each one of you is a part of it.

– (1 Corinthians 12:27 NIV) –

CHAPTER EIGHTEEN

CHRIST-LIKE LEADERSHIP

*But whoever would be great among you must be
your servant, and whoever would be first among
you must be your slave, even as the Son of Man
came not to be served but to serve, and to
give his life as a ransom for many.*

– (Matthew 20:26-28 ESV) –

My five- and six-year-old granddaughters adore playing house. The older always likes to be the mommy and the younger normally complies. However, one day, having had her fill of being the baby in their pretend world, the younger one decided she wanted to be the mommy for once. Her older sister thought about it for a moment, smiled, and finally said, "Okay. You can be the mommy and I will be the grandma!" I had to smile when I heard this story. She was still attempting to be the one in charge!

Sadly, that same kind of desire for control affects many adults in positions of authority and often it negatively affects their style of leadership. Jesus taught a style of leadership that is not about control, nor is it about power. In fact, Jesus exemplified a way to manage that is completely opposite of the world's way of thinking.

Ken Blanchard is one of the greatest authorities on leadership and management in modern times. His book, *One Minute Manager*, has been translated into thirty-seven languages and over 13,000,000 copies have been sold. Years after Ken Blanchard wrote this powerful book, he appeared on Hour of Power with Robert Schuller. Dr. Schuller commended Ken for his writing of *One Minute Manager* and asked him if he knew who the greatest one-minute manager of all time was. "No, who is that?" Ken responded. "Jesus Christ," Dr. Schuller replied. Dr. Schuller then began to reflect on the main points of Ken's book, noting how Jesus perfectly exemplified each one. Not long after that, Ken Blanchard gave his life to the Lord and later wrote *Lead Like Jesus*. He was quoted as saying, "The more I read the Bible, the more evident it becomes that everything I have ever taught or written about effective leadership over the past twenty-five years, Jesus did with perfection. He is simply the greatest leadership role model of all time."[11] So it is in the life of Jesus we find the greatest leadership principles.

For one, Jesus led by example and encouraged the disciples to do the same. 1 Timothy 4:12 (ESV) says in part: ". . . *but set the believers an example in speech, in conduct, in love, in faith, in purity.*" When I was growing up, it wasn't uncommon to hear adults jokingly say, "Do as I say, not as I do." But Jesus taught the opposite of that. Peter exhorted followers of Jesus in this way: "*Christ, who suffered for you, is your example. Follow in his steps: He never sinned, never told a lie, never answered back when insulted; when he suffered he did not threaten to get even; he left his case in the hands of God who always judges fairly*" (1 Peter 2:21–23 TLB). The most effective leaders I have known in my lifetime are those who never asked their people to do what they would be unwilling to do themselves. Granted, each member of the body has a different role, and the leader can't always engage

---

11. Kenneth H. Blanchard and Phil Hodges, *Lead Like Jesus: Lessons from the Greatest Leadership Role Model of All Times* (Nashville, TN: W Pub. Group, 2005).

in all the tasks they need others to do. But there should always be a sense of knowing a leader would be in the trenches along with their people if the need presented itself.

Jesus also led with humility. I once heard humility defined as the ability to recognize who you are in relation to who God is. When leading with humility, there is a constant awareness of our own inadequacies and a heightened sensitivity to our need for the strength, wisdom, and provisions only available through our Heavenly Father. Jesus was God in the flesh, and yet even Jesus was a living reflection of humility.

He was also a perfect picture of a willing servant. He constantly demonstrated a heart to serve rather than be served. This was poignantly illustrated when He washed the feet of His disciples. John 13:3–5 (ESV) beautifully captures the moment:

> *Jesus, knowing that the Father had given all things into his hands, and that he had come from God and was going back to God, rose from supper. He laid aside his outer garments, and taking a towel, tied it around his waist. Then he poured water into a basin and began to wash the disciples' feet and to wipe them with the towel that was wrapped around him.*

When He was finished, He instructed them to do the same, modeling not only servanthood but leading by example as well.

As we study the life of Christ, we see He also led with grace. He always responded with utmost care and concern for others regardless of what could have seemed like countless distractions. The woman with the issue of blood touching the hem of His garment at Capernaum (Matthew 9:20–22), the leper in Galilee (Matthew 8:1–4), and the blind man at Bethsaida (Mark 8:22–26) are but a few. During these and numerous other times in the life of Jesus, we see people begging for His attention. Surely, He had to have grown weary from all the demands, yet He was even willing to take time for the children. *"But Jesus called the children to him and said, 'Let the little children come to me, and do not hinder them, for the kingdom of God belongs to such as these'"* (Luke 18:16 NIV). What an inspiration to each of us not to grow weary from the demands of our work.

> *It is in the life of Jesus Christ we find the greatest leadership principles.*

In addition, Christ-inspired leadership means treating all people fairly and with love. Jesus demonstrated this repeatedly as He reached out to the poor, those with physical limitations and those shunned by society. Whether it was the woman caught in an adulterous relationship or the paralyzed man, Jesus responded to each with tenderness and compassion. As leaders, we must respond to all those in our charge and with whom we come in contact with the same sensitivity and care.

Though Jesus responded with love to anyone and everyone who approached Him, He also knew the importance of drawing away to spend time with His Father. He knew the value of rest and taught us how vital it is that we spend time in quiet, simply seeking the face of God, entering into fellowship with Him, worshiping Him and basking in His presence.

Another important leadership quality Jesus modeled is the principle of delegating. Matthew 14:15–20 (NIV) wonderfully relates one of the many times Jesus delegated to those He was mentoring.

> *As evening approached, the disciples came to him and said, "This is a remote place, and it's already getting late. Send the crowds away, so they can go to the villages and buy themselves some food." Jesus replied, "They do not need to go away. You give them something to eat." "We have here only five loaves of bread and two fish," they answered. "Bring them here to me," he said. And he directed the people to sit down on the*

*grass. Taking the five loaves and the two fish and look-
ing up to heaven, he gave thanks and broke the loaves.
Then he gave them to the disciples, and the disciples
gave them to the people. All ate and were satisfied,
and the disciples picked up twelve basketfuls of broken
pieces that were left over.*

One of my favorite expressions about delegation is: delegate
what others can do so that you can do what only you can do. This
was exactly what Jesus was doing. Jesus performed the miracle of
multiplying the loaves and fishes and then He delegated to His
disciples the distribution of the nourishment and the gathering
of the leftovers.

Toward the latter part of His earthly ministry, Jesus told the
disciples to go out and share the good news of the gospel to all
nations. He equipped them to do the work and then left them
to carry out the mission. There is no substitute for learning how
to delegate in this way. If Jesus recognized the need for it, we, as
Christian leaders, must as well.

Jesus also demonstrated the importance of training up future
leaders. Talk about mentorship! Christ spent twenty-four hours a
day, seven days a week for three years investing in the twelve men
who would spread the good news He was put on this earth to
bring. First, He got to know them, really know them. He gained
an understanding of each of them, their likes and dislikes, their
strengths and their weaknesses. He used everyday situations to
teach them. He also used parables and allegories which they
could relate to. He befriended them. He coached them and
counseled them. He sometimes rebuked them and He never gave
up on them. When He knew they were ready, He gave them the
power and the authority to fulfill their God-given mission. As
strong leaders, it is imperative we follow His example, raising up
those who can follow in our footsteps and continue carrying out
whatever work God has called us to do.

I've heard there are two kinds of leadership: leadership by

intimidation and leadership by inspiration. Jesus modeled the latter, and to be effective Christians in leadership, we must pattern ourselves after Him. As we practice His Biblical principles of leadership, I believe people will be drawn to the Jesus they see in us. When you think about it, isn't that the highest and most important responsibility for any Godly leader? To live and lead in such a way, people are drawn to Christ!

And you who are bosses, be good to your servants
also. Do not talk loud, hard words to them.
Remember that both their Lord and yours is in
heaven. He does not love one person more
than another.

– (Ephesians 6:8 WE) –

CHAPTER NINETEEN

THE GENTLE CHISEL

*Bondservants, obey your earthly masters with fear
and trembling, with a sincere heart, as you would
Christ, not by the way of eye-service, as people-
pleasers, but as bondservants of Christ, doing
the will of God from the heart, rendering service
with a good will as to the Lord and not to man,
knowing that whatever good anyone does, this
he will receive back from the Lord, whether he is
a bondservant or is free. Masters, do the same to
them, and stop your threatening, knowing that he
who is both their Master and yours is in heaven,
and that there is no partiality with him.*

– (Ephesians 6:5-9 ESV) –

From the onset of the Little Light House, I found myself
bearing the responsibility of being the one "in charge."
With no preparation, I had been suddenly thrown into
the position of having to head up a developmental center for
children with special needs, a field in which I had absolutely

no background. I was thrilled with the exponential growth the Little Light House was experiencing, but inside I was in great turmoil. I knew I needed to step up to the plate as the supervisor to the staff, but I had next-to-no supervisory or administrative experience.

I didn't feel I had the respect of the staff and the families we served. Being so close in age made the situation even more difficult. I felt constantly challenged by staff members regarding my decisions and those made by our Board of Directors. All of this resulted in my confidence reaching a lifetime low.

I felt weak and indecisive, and things were getting worse instead of better. I knew God was speaking to my heart, directing my steps; but when my actions and decisions were questioned, I would weaken and doubt God and myself. The staff I was working with was made up of amazing young women who were passionate about serving Christ. They were young and zealous. This was the first job for most of them. All of these factors combined to create a situation in which I felt completely inadequate to lead them. As things continued to worsen, I began to wonder if I should perhaps resign.

I was contemplating that very idea one evening as I left the office and headed to the parking lot. I was just about to get in my car when one of our teachers called to me. We chatted about the day for a few minutes and then she said something to me that was life-changing. She said, "Marcia, I just want to let you know, I trust God's ability to work through you." I don't recall what my visible reaction was at the time, but those words had a dramatic impact and made my heart take flight. I hugged her and thanked her, and then we both went our separate ways for the evening.

All the way home I pondered her words. She trusted God's ability to work through me. It was an "aha" moment for me as I turned over in my mind the realization I wasn't really the one in charge. God was in charge. I was just His vessel. I didn't need to believe in myself. I just needed to believe in God and trust His ability to work through me. I likened it to a water hose, which doesn't have to do much except allow the water to flow through it.

It is important for God's people to trust in His ability to work through those He places in leadership.

The next day, I walked in with a new sense of confidence and assurance. The staff seemed to recognize the difference in me and within a short period of time, I felt the dynamics of our relationship changing for the good. They, too, seemed to be trusting God's ability to speak and work through me.

I'm sure the Israelites had problems trusting in Moses, but they saw God's power revealed through him. In his own strength, Moses could do nothing. But with God working through him, he was able to lead the people with the authority God had given him. All of this points to the importance of God's people trusting in God's ability to work through those He places in leadership.

He also calls us to submit to those He has placed in authority over us. They typically have a different perspective than those who are in submission to them. Good leaders are constantly monitoring the whole picture, where those in submission are often only able to view one part of the picture.

There are times when those in authority are not at liberty to reveal all the information they are privy to for reasons of confidentiality and/or respect for individuals involved. This is just one of the many reasons why staff members should pray for those in authority and submit with a sincere heart.

Another interesting observation I have made over the years is that those who consistently exhibit a teachable, moldable spirit grow and mature into model staff members. It has also been my observation that those who consistently resist correction and are not open to coaching tend to flounder, failing to mature personally and professionally.

Years ago, a spiritual growth seminar I attended focused a significant part of its teachings on chain of command. The speaker shared an illustration I've never forgotten. He held up a sketch of a large, rough rock. Over the rock, you could see the master's hands, one of which was holding a chisel over the rock; the other, a hammer over the chisel, poised to chip away at the rock according to his plan. The next image showed the results of the chisel having cut away a portion of the rock revealing a diamond or bright gem. While hidden within the rock, the gem could not shine; but when subject to the master's hand and chisel, the gem was exposed. The presenter went on to teach that when we subject ourselves to correction from an authority, we are allowing God to work through that authority to chip away at that which keeps us from shining for Him. From my own life experiences, I know this to be true.

When we fail to allow God to work through those in authority over us, oftentimes God will move us under another authority who will be more likely able to shape us. I well recall another illustration about a young boy who was frustrated with his parents telling him what to do, making him rise early in the morning, clean his room, and make his bed before he was ready. He finally spouted off to them, "I've had it with you telling me what to do all the time. I'm going to join the Army!" Whoa! That young boy was about to meet the chisel of his lifetime! The Bible tells us, "*Whosoever loves instruction loves knowledge: but he that hates reproof is senseless*" (Proverbs 12:1 KJ2000).

Personally speaking, some of the best guidance, direction, and correction I ever received was from board chairmen whom God placed in a position of authority over me. It wasn't always "easy listening," but they taught me volumes about how to supervise in a Godly way and redirect staff with a gentle kind of strength. I still made many mistakes, but I will be forever grateful to those faithful men and women who taught me by example and gently nurtured leadership qualities in me which I would never have learned any other way.

God does work through authorities, and unless we are asked to do something immoral, unbiblical, or illegal, we are to submit to authority. In so doing, we will allow God's hand to work through His chosen chisel and expose the diamond in us.

> *Obey them that have the rule over you, and submit*
> *yourselves: for they watch for your souls, as they*
> *that must give account, that they may do it with*
> *joy, and not with grief: for that is unprofitable*
> *for you.*

— (Hebrews 13:17 KJV) —

CHAPTER TWENTY

AN OPEN BOOK

Consequently, each of us will give an account of
himself to God.

– (Romans 14:12 ISV) –

A nd the award goes to . . . the Little Light House!"
Applause rang out across the room as other members of
the Little Light House staff joined me, rising to our feet
and making our way to the podium. It was a large room so it took
a minute to reach the front. As we gazed at that beautiful award,
we could hardly believe our eyes. But there before us were the
words: "Presented to The Little Light House, 2003 Outstanding
School of the Year."

After a short acceptance speech, we settled back down at our
banquet table. I looked around at the faces of the people who
had helped us get to this point, staff members who had poured
so much into helping us become accredited by this wonderful
association. We were grateful beyond words. It had been a long
journey. We were already so thankful to have been accredited by
the International Christian Accrediting Association. And then to

be honored by such an award from them, only a few years after receiving our accreditation, was beyond our wildest dreams. Such a blessing had to be from God!

For decades before, because we were not a state-certified school, the teaching experience our teachers acquired at the Little Light House wasn't recognized. We had appealed to the State Department of Education in every way we knew but to no avail. We were a preschool for infants and children. There was no agency which offered accreditation to an organization like ours, especially considering the fact our student population was completely made up of children with special needs. We continued to pray and out of the blue, God divinely intervened. The head of the International Christian Accrediting Association contacted us and requested a tour of our center for himself and his colleague. Following the tour, they asked if we ever had considered accreditation. Considered it? We had prayed for it! We couldn't believe our ears.

Accountability is essential to keep us stretching toward excellence.

We explained our plight and told them about our repeated attempts at finding an association that would offer standards applicable to a center like ours. Typically, accrediting programs are geared to elementary, middle, and high schools. Their standards for classroom ratios, extra-curricular activities, and even their building requirements differed dramatically from ours.

A standard for one of these schools might be to have no more than twenty-five students in a classroom with one teacher. For our children, many of whom were medically fragile, developmentally delayed and oftentimes unable to walk or even sit up on their own, such a standard would be completely inappropriate. Our standard would need to be a fraction of that number of students for each teacher if we were going to be effective. The standards simply didn't line up with our type of school.

The ICAA representatives understood these factors completely but, for some reason known only to God, they wanted to find a way to make it work. They wanted us to be a part of their association and offered to adapt their guidelines to accommodate the unique aspects of a school like ours. We were thrilled! We had finally found an accrediting association to which we could hold ourselves accountable. In addition to that, a stamp of endorsement from an international accrediting association like ICAA would provide validation of the Little Light House to our state, our nation, and to the entire world.

A number of people (even board and staff members) asked why we needed to become accredited. "After all," they'd say, "our children likely won't need to count their preschool experience toward credits for college. So why does the Little Light House need to be accredited?" At the time, we simply believed it was God-directed. We knew it would have value for us but we had no way of knowing to what extent. ICAA provides the best definition of the meaning of accreditation:

> *The word accredited comes from the same root word as credible (to believe or trust). Accreditation, therefore, acknowledges a school's credibility—its believability. Although some might see an accrediting agency as giving credibility to a school, in actuality the process of accreditation ascertains and acknowledges the school's credibility by providing external witnesses.*[12]

There was no question God had orchestrated this opportunity to partner with ICAA and come into alignment with Hebrews 10:24–25 (ESV): "*And let us consider how to stir up one another to love and good works, not neglecting to meet together, as is the habit of some, but encouraging one another, and all the more as you see the Day drawing near.*" God had raised up a wonderful Christian agency to encourage us, help us, and urge us toward

---

12. See http://icaa.us/accrediting-information/.

excellence in our service to the Lord. A number of additional meetings took place between our Little Light House staff and the leadership of ICAA. Soon we began the arduous two-year process of preparing for their site visits. ICAA representatives would be invited to come in and view every aspect of the ministry's programs and operation.

To be accountable, we must be willing to be vulnerable, an open book, of sorts; but doing so reaps great rewards. Being vulnerable in this case meant beginning the long, hard process of preparing for the site visit. Literally every aspect of every component of the Little Light House would be assessed to determine if we were up to the ICAA level of excellence. If the site team came for their visit and found us deficient in certain areas, we would be given a designated amount of time to make the necessary changes. If they were made during that time limit, we'd be recommended for accreditation. If not, we wouldn't be, and we would have to wait another year to attempt the process again.

For two years, notebooks were compiled, one for each area of standards: facility and grounds, administration and operations, finances, educational program, staff records and credentials, historical records, and opportunities offered to our staff for spiritual, personal, and professional growth. Each area would be subject to evaluation. We worked at a feverish pace preparing for our site visit. We wanted desperately to go above and beyond since they were so willing to adjust their standards to make them appropriate for our type of school. We reorganized and updated files, addressed leaks in our roof, and tackled other facility problems. We completed endless forms and dug through archives to locate historical documents which had been requested. Our staff credentials were carefully reviewed and every aspect of our operation was reevaluated and revised for maximum efficiency and effectiveness.

Every staff member participated to one degree or another and various staff members were put in charge of different areas of concentration. When the deadline came and the visitors arrived, seven huge notebooks with clearly labeled tabs and perfectly organized contents sat ready for inspection!

Our ICAA site team members were gracious, kind, and very affirming. Their three-day visit passed quickly and at the end, they met with the entire staff to summarize their findings. Their final report recommended us for accreditation without exception. We were jubilant! All of our hard work had paid off. We had placed ourselves in an accountable position to Christian brothers and sisters and my, how God honored our act of obedience.

To begin with, because of their affiliation with the State Department of Education, our teachers' years of experience at the Little Light House became recognized as valid tenure. Professionals in related fields began to put more credence in our services.

At their annual meeting, when all of the ICAA accredited schools gathered in Tulsa from all over the world, the ICAA leadership recognized the Little Light House and invited us to speak to the entire assembly, advocating for children with special needs. In fact, they went on to invite me to speak to additional conferences being held in Costa Rica, Mexico, and Fort Worth which raised awareness of the needs and potential of children with disabilities. Lasting relationships were formed with representatives from across the globe.

There are other areas where the Little Light House has benefited from voluntarily making ourselves accountable. Decades ago, we realized the importance of arranging to have financial audits conducted on an annual basis. Though the process is costly, the benefits of receiving the trust of the community far outweigh every penny invested.

There are also areas of accountability which the government mandates such as federal, state, and city regulations regarding health, safety, and licensing. I believe God would have us welcome their inspections and reviews. Though they may seem inconvenient at times, these are regulations which keep our students, volunteers, and staff safe and out of harm's way.

In addition, we have always believed that because God works through untold numbers of people in the community, we should also hold ourselves accountable to our constituents and the families we serve. Therefore, we are committed to providing opportunities to allow them to see firsthand the work that goes on at the Little Light House. For that reason, every classroom offers observation windows, and tours are led daily so interested people from the community and parents of Little Light House children can see our program in action. The Little Light House also hosts community luncheons throughout the year inviting friends, neighbors, church leaders, and others to tour the center and learn more about our mission and vision over a complimentary lunch.

In addition, accountability reports from every department of the ministry are submitted to the Little Light House Board of Directors on a bi-monthly basis. These are then reviewed by the board and must be approved.

Accountability is critical at every level and for every walk of life. For corporations, ministries, churches, and even in our personal lives, accountability is essential to keep us stretching, growing, and moving toward excellence. It is in this excellence that God is glorified and our mission is fulfilled.

> *If you are faithful in little things, you will be faithful in large ones. But if you are dishonest in little things, you won't be honest with greater responsibilities. And if you are untrustworthy about worldly wealth, who will trust you with the true riches of heaven? And if you are not faithful with other people's things, why should you be trusted with things of your own?*
>
> – (Luke 16:10-12 NLT) –

CHAPTER TWENTY-ONE

FIRST THINGS FIRST

*But seek ye first the kingdom of God, and his
righteousness; and all these things shall be added
unto you.*

– (Matthew 6:33 KJV) –

The in-depth study of our foundational Scripture, detailed
in an earlier chapter, inspired the mission statement for
our center: "To glorify God by improving the quality of life
for children with special needs, their families and communities."
Our focus on the scriptural mandate to *"Let your light so shine
before men, that they may see your good works and glorify your
Father in heaven,"* led us to recognize the calling on our center to
be a ministry of light.

But how does one go about being a ministry of light in a dark
world? God's answer to that question is found in Matthew 6:33
(KJV). *"Seek ye first the kingdom of God and his righteousness,
and all these things shall be added unto you."* God is telling us, as
we put Him first and always strive to further His kingdom and
bring Him glory, He will take care of the rest.

> *The question must always be asked, "Are we putting God's kingdom and His righteousness first?"*

Therefore, it has long been my conviction, and that of our Board of Directors and staff, if we want to provide the best possible services to the children and families we serve, our first commitment must be to put God first. This has served as the guiding principle for all decisions made by the leadership of the Little Light House. Regardless of whether they are large decisions or small ones, and regardless of how tempting it might be to compromise, the question must always be asked: are we putting God's kingdom and His righteousness first? If not, we must stop and pray until we are sure we are ready to do His work—His way—to His glory.

God has always honored our obedience to this very important Biblical principle. The first time He etched this truth in our hearts took place in the earlier years. A likable and well-known gentleman in the community was going to be opening a new restaurant in Tulsa. He had approached us about endorsing and helping to host a grand opening of this restaurant. He, in turn, would allow the proceeds to benefit the Little Light House. Of course, we were thrilled. We were greatly in need of the revenue. When we met with him at the restaurant, however, we noticed there was a liquor bar. We inquired as to whether they would have the bar open the evening of the event. We explained our policy which prevented us, as a Christian ministry, from assisting with a fund-raising project if alcohol was served. I knew I couldn't make an exception because, based on Scripture, we believed we were not to participate in any activity which could cause someone to stumble. This conviction was based on Romans 14:13–23 (ESV) which states in part: *"Therefore, let us not pass judgment on one another any longer, but rather decide never to put a stumbling block or hindrance in the way of a brother. . . . It is good not to eat meat or drink wine or do anything that causes your brother to stumble.*" The restaurant owner was a bit taken aback by our policy, but readily agreed to keep the bar closed for that one evening.

The night of the event arrived. We had publicized it to our donors, and our staff and Board of Directors were all on hand to serve as hosts. The evening started off great. The food was superb and everyone seemed to be enjoying themselves. The event was very well attended and our board and staff were delighted with the turnout.

However, half-way through the evening, several reporters from the media arrived and began to apply pressure on the owner to open the bar. He complied. Several of our donors were a bit surprised and disappointed to see alcohol being served at a Little Light House event which, from all due appearances, the function seemed to be.

We apologized to the offended donors and tried to make the best of an awkward and difficult situation. When it was over, we tried to keep our focus on the heart of this kind businessman who had genuinely wanted to make a difference in the lives of our children. We graciously thanked him for his efforts and the financial contributions which had resulted from the evening. God went before us and preserved relationships with both the restaurant owner and our donors. We knew, however, we had potentially compromised our witness for Christ to those in attendance.

A few years later, the same gentleman was getting ready to open another restaurant (and bar) and contacted me about once again benefitting the Little Light House. As before, he wanted us to invite all of our support base and assist with the event. I thanked him for his offer and asked if they would be opening the bar. He chuckled and said "yes," and explained he would need to do so. It was a difficult moment. I knew we desperately needed the revenue, but I also knew that as a Christian ministry we had decided it could compromise our witness for Christ to be a part of an event which served alcohol. I explained this to him, thanked him for thinking of us and, as diplomatically as I was able, turned down his offer. It was a hard move, but I genuinely felt God was speaking to my heart and saying I had done the right thing. I was simply to trust the Lord and He would provide in other ways. Sure enough, a short time later, a large donation came in from a completely unexpected source. It was for the very amount we likely would have received if we had participated in the restaurant's grand opening.

This scenario has played out time and again. When we first began hosting a golf tournament benefitting the Little Light House, we were told it would never succeed if we didn't allow alcohol on the course. We stood our ground, maintained our commitment, and years later, our golf tournament is considered one of the most popular in our city.

One point of clarification: we are in no way standing in judgment of those who drink or serve alcoholic beverages. Likely there are those on our board and staff who on occasion will have a glass of wine. But as a Christian ministry, we believe God has impressed upon us that we are to be above reproach and even above question. If there is anything which might raise a question about our corporate witness, we will never knowingly do it. This has also meant not conducting raffles, even though they may be a popular means of fund-raising. Since raffles could conceivably be considered a form of gambling—and gambling, like alcohol, has ruined countless lives—this is something we believe we are not to do. In other words, as representatives of our Lord Jesus Christ, we don't want to knowingly set an example which could lead anyone down a path of destruction.

For some, these viewpoints may seem radical; however, it has been the path God has impressed the Little Light House to follow and we believe He has honored it. If we err, we err on the side of caution so we can be sure we are in no way compromising our witness for Christ. Undoubtedly, there have been times we have missed the mark, but it is our heart's intent to do nothing which would dim the light of our mission. What a comfort to know, as we seek first the righteousness of God, He will bless our efforts and make a way for the completion of the work we are doing in His name.

> *In everything you do, put God first, and he will*
> *direct you and crown your efforts with success.*

– (Proverbs 3:6 TLB) –

CHAPTER TWENTY-TWO

DIVINE FINANCES

*And it is he who will supply all your needs from
his riches in glory because of what Christ Jesus has
done for us.*

– (Philippians 4:19 TLB) –

Often it is delegates from other nations who pose the question. On other occasions, it comes from business professionals, ministers, or other community leaders. Sometimes we have a microphone in front of us as reporters ask: "How are you funded?"

We love this question because it gives us the opportunity to tell others about the loving God we serve. We are happy to report, as we have individually and corporately trusted God for more than four decades, He has provided for every need of the Little Light House. We've never known exactly how this would be accomplished. But the provision has always been there. We learned the difference between want and need over the years and sometimes the provision was delayed until God knew we were really ready for it. But He has always provided.

People are typically stunned and puzzled when they learn the Little Light House does not charge for any of the services rendered. This has probably been the cause of more questions and head-scratching than any other aspect of the ministry. As CEO, I was frequently asked what our major source of revenue was, and how we were able to manage without the benefit of state or federal funds, United Way funding, or insurance reimbursements. I could only answer one way: by the grace and power of God.

In the beginning, responding to some well-intended advice, we had charged ten dollars a month tuition. However, when we entered into the three-year agreement with public schools a year later, we dropped even that small tuition and forever thereafter provided the services tuition-free. God impressed upon our hearts the services were to be a ministry. He also provided scriptural confirmation in Philippians 4:19 as well as confirmation from the Holy Spirit that He would continue to meet all of the needs of our center. But I often wondered how even God Himself could keep up with the growing financial obligations of the Little Light House. There was no way I could even imagine all God had in store for the future. I couldn't begin to fathom the miraculous provision we would witness in the years to come, or how God would teach us volumes about His divine finance principles. Over time, God used a number of factors and influences to shape us and show us how the Little Light House was to operate.

In the early years, George Müller's life and story had a profound impact on me. George Müller was a Christian evangelist who lived in the eighteenth century. He provided care for over 10,000 orphans, established over 117 schools, and educated over 120,000 children, most of them orphans. Through all of his efforts, Müller never made requests to any man for financial support, nor did he ever go in debt. He set exceptionally high standards for all of his schools and was known for keeping scrupulous accounting of every gift, no matter the size. He completely trusted God for all provisions, regardless of the circumstances. This level of trust was exemplified one morning when Mr. Müller and all of his orphans had gathered for breakfast as was their custom. As always, they bowed their heads in prayer and gave thanks for their food. This particular morning, however, there was no food in the orphanage—none whatsoever. Mr. Müller had led the prayer with faith in His heavenly provider. Moments later, enough fresh bread to feed everyone was delivered by a generous baker. Almost simultaneously, a milk cart broke down in front of the orphanage, and as a result milk was provided for all of the children. Reading about the amazing life and works of this great man strengthened my faith and built my belief that, as we trusted and obeyed God, the needs of the ministry would be met.

Looking back, I can now see clearly the remarkable principles of divine finance God was teaching us. There were several which stood out and allowed His light to shine brighter through us as we learned and developed into the ministry God called us to be.

> *God's work done God's way will not lack God's provision.*

For one, though as a non-profit we didn't have to pay income tax, we did have to pay payroll taxes and we knew we were to pay them promptly and in full. Matthew 22:20–21 (ESV) makes this point clear. *"And Jesus said to them, 'Whose likeness and inscription is this?' They said, 'Caesar's.' Then he said to them, 'Therefore render to Caesar the things that are Caesar's, and to God the things that are God's.'"* This became a Biblical principle to which we have remained fully committed.

In addition, God impressed upon our hearts early on that we were to consistently pay our bills on time and incur no debt. *"Let no debt remain outstanding, except the continuing debt to love one another, for whoever loves others has fulfilled the law"* (Romans 13:8 NIV). We knew it would greatly compromise our witness for Christ if we didn't pay our vendors and businesses promptly what we owed them, so we made it a strong commitment to maintain that Biblical practice.

Knowing how God felt about debt, when it came time to build our first permanent homesite, we wondered how we could possibly construct a 20,000-square-foot facility without acquiring a loan. Still, God made it clear to us we were not to borrow. *"The rich rule over the poor, and the borrower is servant to the lender"* (Proverbs 22:7 NET). Though the temptations were great to secure a loan, we were resolute that we would not go in debt. Psychologically, it was challenging. We had scores of children on the waiting list and we knew it would likely take years for all the funds to be raised. Surely God would want the children to receive services sooner rather than later. Still, we continued to receive confirmation from God we were not to incur debt.

As it turned out, the season of waiting was seven long years between the time God impressed upon our hearts we were to pursue a permanent homesite and the time we occupied our new building. But in the spring of 1990, we moved into our $2.2 million new home, debt-free.

A little over two decades later, the Little Light House had maxed out that facility. Again, we agonized over the waiting list, now even longer. Just as before, the temptations were great to take out a loan. Once more, we remembered the principle God had so strongly impressed upon our hearts and determined we would only build when the funding was in hand to do so. We stayed the course, and in August of 2016, the Little Light House moved into the new 40,000-square-foot addition to our existing building. It was a $16,500,000 project, built debt-free, and the Little Light House operations remained debt-free when the project was completed. There had been no bonds sold and no loans involved. God had simply worked through the obedient hearts of individuals, groups, foundations, and churches throughout the community. They all gave selflessly because of the love and compassion they felt for the precious children we serve and their belief in our mission.

My friends, I don't know about you, but I'd call that a miracle, and such a miracle can only happen in the world of divine finances. It was God's grace and His miraculous power at work through generous people willing to allow God to work through them. We will remain forever grateful for each and every person God used.

From early on we had also dedicated ourselves to being conscientious with our bookkeeping and were committed to maintaining careful records of our financial receipts and spending. "*Riches can disappear fast. And the king's crown doesn't stay in his family forever—so watch your business interests closely. Know the state of your flocks and your herds*" (Proverbs 27:23–24 TLB). We constantly stressed to the staff we were to maintain our supplies and equipment in an organized fashion so as not to duplicate supplies we already had on hand. All too often, organizations purchase materials unnecessarily due to carelessness and a lack of order. This results in the loss of valuable financial resources. "*Now this is what the LORD Almighty says: 'Give careful thought to your ways. . . . You earn wages, only to put them in a purse with holes in it'*" (Haggai 1:5–6 NIV). We carefully avoided wasting any resources we were so thankful to have received. We were called to use every gift wisely, be it in-kind or financial.

When we found ourselves with an overabundance of a particular item as a result of extremely generous donations, we contacted ministries doing a similar work and shared with them. We felt we couldn't with integrity tithe monetary donations which had been given for the children of the Little Light House, but when we found ourselves with more supplies such as crayons, markers, or glue sticks than we could store, we felt we were to share with others who were also meeting the needs of children with challenges. "*See that you . . . excel in this grace of giving*" (2 Corinthians 8:7 NIV).

As the years passed, recognizing we never knew for certain where our revenue was coming from, we worked hard to become more effective at the budgeting process. We set revenue goals and projected our fund-raising yield and specific areas of income. God in His Word had exhorted us to manage our financial affairs wisely, monitor our spending, and project our revenue with great thought and prayer. Of course, we wanted everything for the children—more teachers, social workers, therapists, and better equipment—but we knew God was telling us to operate within our means. I'm grateful to this day for Godly board members who stood firm and did not allow our emotions to run ahead of our better judgment. *"The wise man saves for the future, but the foolish man spends whatever he gets"* (Proverbs 21:20 TLB).

Since the early years of the Little Light House, the needs have grown. By 2016, our budget requirements had soared to a seven-figure total, a far cry from the $3,000 budget we started out with. Yet every need continues to be met. Understanding all of this, one can only conclude, it is by the power and provision of God that the light of the Little Light House continues to shine. It also validates again that God's work, God's way will not lack God's provision. Without adhering to the Biblical principles of finance God laid out for us in His Word, and without the grace and power of God, surely the Little Light House would not be standing today. My friends, I encourage you, consider carefully the Biblical mandates God has given us. They are His loving way of guiding, protecting, and providing for His children. It is what I would call divine finances, which is God's way of helping His people stay the course.

And God is able to make all grace abound toward you; that ye, always having all sufficiency in all things, may abound to every good work.

— (2 Corinthians 9:8 KJV) —

CHAPTER TWENTY-THREE

SURVEYING THE WALL

*For I know the plans I have for you," declares the
LORD, "plans to prosper you and not to harm you,
plans to give you hope and a future. Then you will
call on me and come and pray to me, and I will
listen to you. You will seek me and find me when
you seek me with all your heart.*

– (Jeremiah 29:11-13 NIV) –

Years ago, God brought individuals our way who had
expertise in something they called strategic planning.
I was resistant and struggled with the concept; I even
questioned whether it was a Biblical practice. After all, God's
Word says, *"The heart of man plans his way, but the LORD
establishes his steps"* (Proverbs 16:9 ESV). For years, I had been
inclined to believe we were to let God lead us day by day. After all,
that seemed to have worked during the founding years. Looking
back, I know now . . . it was only by His grace that it worked and
I am grateful.

But as the years went by, I began to realize there is compelling evidence in Scripture that God is an advocate of planning. Though the concept and terminology of strategic planning, mission statements, and vision statements are modern-day concepts, the practice goes all the way back to Bible times.

Nehemiah was a classic example of a man of God who planned strategically. He knew he had a daunting task when God called him to rebuild the walls of Jerusalem. Under God's direction, he surveyed the wall, appraised the damage, assembled his resources, appointed leaders, and delegated assignments.

There are numerous other examples of careful, meticulous strategic planning in the Old and New Testament. Consider how David's life was spared by listening to God's strategic plan to slay Goliath. The strategy involved one stone aimed at the one weak point of the giant he was to fight; this would assure him of certain victory. Paul was strategic in the planning of his missionary journeys, focusing on geographic areas where he could have the greatest impact on the largest populations. God Himself demonstrated the ultimate strategic plan to bring salvation to mankind through the death and resurrection of His only begotten Son.

A strategic plan must be a guide, not a god.

The big difference between the strategic planning process in the secular world and strategic planning for Christian leaders has to do with whether they are man-made plans or God-directed plans. Many forget this key point and tend to make plans on their own. Then they wonder why God doesn't bless them.

Unquestionably, a constant seeking of divine guidance and direction must accompany the entire strategic planning process. Equally important is remembering that a strategic plan must be a guide, not a god. We must always be sensitive to the leadership of the Holy Spirit, as God sometimes redirects or may lead us on detours in order to show us things we might not grasp otherwise.

The Little Light House professional staff devoted more than two decades to developing a Bible-based curriculum which could be used for typical children as well as children with special needs. For the better part of those twenty-plus years, it was an element of our strategic planning that the curriculum would one day provide a healthy revenue stream for the Little Light House. It wasn't until this unique curriculum was completed that God laid it on the hearts of the Little Light House staff and board that the curriculum was to be made available without charge to anyone in the world with a heart to help children with special needs. It was a significant decision that would definitely affect Little Light House income, but God made it clear to the leadership this was His mandate. Without question, the decision has the potential to impact far more children than we likely would have ever imagined.

So not only must our plans be directed by God, we must also be open to His redirection at all times. We would be foolish to want our own plans when we can have the plans of Almighty God who created the universe and everything within it.

God also teaches us in His Word to seek Godly counsel in the strategic planning process. *"Plans fail for lack of counsel, but with many advisers they succeed"* (Proverbs 15:22 NIV). Some of the most valuable insight we ever received was counsel we sought during the strategic planning process. This principle also applies to individuals seeking direction for their own lives. I, for one, will be forever grateful to those men and women who taught, counseled, and coached me throughout the years I was at the helm of the Little Light House ministry. Trust me, whether you are a business leader, a missionary, or a follower of Christ who wants to make a difference in your world, you can glean a treasury of wisdom from life experiences of Godly men and women who know you and care about you and your work.

The process of strategic planning also typically involves assessment of our strengths and areas of weakness once they have been identified. This is a valuable component of the process and is a crucial exercise for any organization. In order to know where we need to grow, we must have an acute awareness of where we are lacking.

No matter what calling God has placed on our lives, these principles of planning must be embraced if we want to be effective in our service to the Lord.

Commit your work to the LORD, and your plans will succeed.

– (Proverbs 16:3 CEB) –

CHAPTER TWENTY-FOUR
A GOOD STEW
TAKES TIME

*Put it in writing, because it is not yet time for it
to come true. But the time is coming quickly, and
what I show you will come true. It may seem slow
in coming, but wait for it; it will certainly take
place, and it will not be delayed.*

– (Habakkuk 2:3 GNT) –

The little girl tugged on her mommy's skirt. "Please, Mommy, I want to taste it now!" The mother smiled as she stirred the homemade stew she was cooking. "Not now, sweetheart. It isn't time yet." The little girl had been watching as her mother peeled and cut up the carrots, onions, and potatoes, adding them to the stew. The aroma had begun to waft through the house, drawing the child into the kitchen. "But Mommy, why can't I taste it now?" The mother bent down and gently cupped the child's chin in her hand. "Well, sweetheart, I could give you some of Mommy's stew now but it wouldn't taste very good." "But why, Mommy? It's got all the stuff in it, doesn't it?" the little one asked. "Well . . . yes," her mother answered, "but you see, it has to cook for a long time. It's the time that makes it so good. Time is probably the most important ingredient!"

Many of us have felt like this little girl. We don't understand why things don't happen more quickly. If it is in God's power, why must we wait? But, just as the stew needs time to reach its full flavor, so do many of life's challenges need time to reach their full resolution. It's a principle that has been in place since the beginning of time itself. God took six days to create the heavens and the earth and then He rested on the seventh.

It takes nine months for a baby to be born. A baby needs those months in the womb to reach a stage of maturity which will allow it to survive outside the mother's womb. It takes a baby chick hours to break out of its shell. All the while, however, the chick is building up the strength it will need once outside of that shell.

Just as good stew needs time to reach its full flavor, so do life's challenges need time to reach their full resolution.

Along the same line, it takes years for a tiny acorn to become a mighty oak tree, but once that acorn has fallen, it begins developing an amazing root system which will keep the tree standing straight and strong for decades. All things take time. It is God's order for things. Still, even knowing this, we remain all too prone to complain when we don't see answers to prayer in the timing we desire.

Such was the case for me when we set out to build the first permanent homesite for the Little Light House, and then again two decades later when we launched the campaign to build the 40,000-square-foot addition to our existing building. Relying one hundred percent on donations, we knew we would have to build debt-free. In both building campaigns, it was seven long years before we were able to break ground.

It was a painful wait. In both cases, the list of children having to wait to be enrolled was long. When we launched the expansion campaign, more than 160 families were desperately wanting and needing services for their children. The wait for enrollment for each child was two to three years.

It was hard for myself and for others to understand. After all, the first six years of life are the most important learning years a child ever experiences. The years these children were having to go without services were critical. I often reasoned with God. Surely He knew their needs. Surely He didn't want them to go with their educational and therapeutic needs unmet.

The amount of money needed in both building campaigns would require God's miracle-working power for sure. But we knew God was still in the miracle-working business. So why the wait? As I pondered this question, the Lord reminded me of the roots of that mighty oak tree I mentioned earlier.

Without that elaborate root system that goes deep into the soil, the oak tree would not withstand the winds and storms of time. As God impressed this on my heart, I began to consider all that had happened over the seven-year season prior to each ground-breaking. As we applied for grants, new foundations became aware of our work. The Little Light House support base broadened and the level of community awareness was heightened. Little Light House programs and procedures were improved, positioning the Little Light House for the growth which would take place in the years to come. I believe God knew all these factors needed to take root in order for the Little Light House to thrive in the face of increasing student populations and a soaring budget.

We can only speculate why God has us wait. We never have to speculate, however, about God knowing what is best for us.

My daughter experienced a painful wait in her late thirties. She had never married. Mr. Right had just never come along, but she wanted very much to be a mommy. After accompanying me on a trip to Beijing, her heart ached to adopt a child from China. However, the Chinese laws did not allow for single parent adoption. We agreed in prayer for either a husband for her or for the Chinese laws to change. We waited for two long years before God answered. It was then we learned that, miraculously, the Chinese laws had in fact been changed. Immediately upon hearing this, she applied to adopt a child. Nine months later, we accompanied her to China to bring back a beautiful little girl, her new daughter. Our daughter later reflected. "You know, Mom. She's the perfect little girl for me. When I first prayed, she hadn't even been born. God definitely knew best." Two years later she returned for still another precious little girl from China and the two, only eight months apart, look so much alike, we are continually asked if they are twins. Both are constant reminders of God's miracle-working power and His perfect timing.

It isn't always easy to wait. It does make it easier, though, as we ponder the fact that God made us and ultimately knows what is best for us. While we are waiting, we must trust. Babbie Mason wrote a beautiful song years ago. The words to the chorus are ones we need to remember.

> *God is too wise to be mistaken.*
> *God is too good to be unkind.*
> *So when you don't understand,*
> *When you don't see His plan,*
> *When you can't trace His hand,*
> *Trust His Heart.*[13]

Trusting eases the pain of waiting. God's timing may not be ours, but it is always in our best interest. When we are passionate about furthering the kingdom of God, impatience can threaten to get the best of us. In those times, to be effective in ministry, we must remember God's timing is perfect and it is in His timing, we must rest and trust.

> *Everything that happens in this world happens at*
> *the time God chooses.*
> *— (Ecclesiastes 3:1 GNT) —*

---

13 "Trust His Heart," written by Babbie Y. Mason and Eddie Carswell, © Warner/Chappell Music, Inc.

CHAPTER TWENTY-FIVE

AN AUDIENCE OF ONE

Whatever you do, do your work heartily, as for the
Lord rather than for men, knowing that from the
Lord you will receive the reward of the inheritance.
It is the Lord Christ whom you serve.

– (Colossians 3:23-24 NASB) –

E ach year the Little Light House holds an event called Laps for Little Ones. It is one of the largest fund-raising events we conduct. It is also one of the most heartwarming as people of all ages gather from Tulsa and surrounding communities for one sole purpose: to make a difference in the lives of children with special needs. The early morning air is always buzzing with excitement. Loud, upbeat music fills the stadium and brightly colored balloons surrounding the track wave wildly in the breeze. The bleachers fill up with friends and family who have come to watch more than 100 participants run so that Little Light House kids might one day walk and talk and experience other remarkable milestones.

The morning begins as all the runners take their mark. The national anthem is sung and a prayer is lifted up. The starting gun is then fired and the large mass of runners take off. It is a sight that always stirs my heart as I behold the many caring people who give up their morning out of a heart for others. Prior to that day, each participant has worked hard to raise sponsorships. Some have secured fixed pledges which designate a set amount to be donated regardless of how many laps the participant runs. Others run for a pledged amount per lap.

There are always a number of serious athletes who never let up from beginning to end. But there are many who seem to just love strolling around the outside track with one or two friends for the duration of the one-hour run.

For decades, I've had the privilege of co-emceeing the event, giving me a ringside seat as the track stars blaze a trail and others move at their leisurely pace. Many of the little tykes take off like gangbusters, but by the time they are half-way through the first quarter mile lap, they are worn out and have slowed their pace to a walk. Then, to my amusement, when they finally get close to the part of the track that wraps in front of the spectators' cheering section, they break into a full sprint. Of course, this always captures the attention of those in the stands, prompting bursts of applause as well as shouts of "Way to go!" and "You're looking great!" You can see pride sweep across their little faces as they cast a quick grin up toward the stands and speed on. Once out of the view of the spectators, they slow their pace down again, catch their breath, and resume a slower gait. This routine is repeated by these little guys and gals time and again throughout the run.

I always get a chuckle from these cute kids but, at the same time, they bring to mind a very important principle. We, too, have a tendency to slow down our pace when we think no one is watching. We often look far too much for the approval and applause of others and fail to remember, we really need only run for an audience of One.

God reminds us of this very important principle in His Word: *"Servants, be obedient to them that are your masters according to the flesh, with fear and trembling, in singleness of your heart, as unto Christ; Not with eyeservice, as menpleasers; but as the servants of Christ, doing the will of God from the heart; With good will doing service, as to the Lord, and not to men"* (Ephesians 6:5–7 KJV).

In other words, it is fine to want to please our bosses, our spouses, our parents, our coaches, our spiritual mentors,

Our greatest aim must be to please God.

and others who are important in our lives. But our greatest aim must be to please God. For in so doing, we will be fulfilling our greatest mission in life. John Wooden, a highly respected coach, once said, "The true test of a man's character is what he does when no one is looking."

My granddaughters, even at the ages of five and six, are gaining an understanding of this truth. They have a few little household chores they are responsible for. One is to clean up their playroom. My daughter likes to nurture the kind of self-discipline required for such a task. She'll often get them started and then leave them alone to complete the job. The tots always start out well, but thinking their mommy isn't watching, our little grand-dolls will allow themselves to get distracted by the very toys they are supposed to be putting away. Before they even realize it, they are giggling and completely caught up once again in a world of pretend and fun, creating an even bigger mess than they started with. Funny though, when they hear their mommy's footsteps, they hop to it and back to work they go. Little do they know, their mommy has a monitor and can view everything going on in their playroom.

God doesn't need a monitor. He knows our hearts, our motives, and is aware of every moment of our day. He knows when we are doing our best and when we are failing Him and letting ourselves down. He is also fully aware when we let ourselves get caught up in doing the very things we never intended to do.

But when we are primarily focused on pleasing our Almighty Lord, we are prompted to make every effort to do our best at all times. We make the kind of decisions God would have us make. We live as He would have us live. We operate with utmost integrity.

When we play to a divine audience of One, our work and our lives will be consistent whether anyone else is watching or not. I like to call people with this kind of aim, God-pleasers.

God-pleasers are at work on time. They are honest in all transactions and fair in their dealings with others. They give maximum effort, 100% of the time. They don't call in sick unless they really are. They don't mind working overtime when their other God-given responsibilities allow them to. They don't let professional jealousy damage working relationships and they put the interest of others before their own. They are good team members and good team builders, cheering on the efforts of others and rejoicing when others are promoted. They believe in improving themselves and developing their God-given talents.

I recognize that all of this may sound like a lot to strive for, but once again, as Christians, we are called to a different set of standards. Hebrews 12:1–2 (NIV) describes the life quest for God-pleasers in this way: "*Therefore, since we are surrounded by such a great cloud of witnesses, let us throw off everything that hinders and the sin that so easily entangles. And let us run with perseverance the race marked out for us, fixing our eyes on Jesus, the pioneer and perfecter of faith. For the joy set before him he endured the cross, scorning its shame, and sat down at the right hand of the throne of God.*"

There is indeed a race marked out for each of us and, as we fix our eyes on Jesus, our race will be run with integrity. It is our Heavenly Father who keeps us on track and reveals to us when we get off course. As we listen to that still, small voice leading us back to His way and urging us on to the path of His will, we are able to keep the faith and focus on the only finish line that matters: that moment we would hear our audience of One say, "Well done, good and faithful servant. Well done." That is far better than any earthly applause we could ever receive, and a true reflection of doing God's work—God's way.

> *For am I now seeking the favor of men, or of God?*
> *Or am I striving to please men? If I were still trying*
> *to please men, I would not be a bond-servant of*
> *Christ.*

— (Galatians 1:10 NASB) —

EPILOGUE

The large door quietly slid open and I stepped inside the spacious elevator in the newly opened Little Light House expansion. I was alone with my thoughts as the door automatically closed. On the wall beside me hung a professionally printed signboard with the Little Light House logo at the top. Listed below the colorful logo were the goals for each department of the ministry. I gazed at the piece and tried to take in all that the moment held. It seemed inconceivable to me. I was actually on a Little Light House elevator. It had only recently been made operational in our new 16.5 million dollar expansion. It all seemed surreal. As the elevator began to move, all I could think about was the tiny frame house which had served as the first Little Light House location more than forty years ago, in 1972. One of the rooms of the small structure would have just fit in that elevator. In fact the entire place could easily have fit in one single classroom of the new facility.

It was staggering to think how much had happened over those four decades since the founding. Our daughter, Missy, had grown up during that time, obtained her Master's degree, and though technically legally blind, was able to get a driver's license at the age of thirty-two, thanks to modern technology involving state-of-the-art contact lenses. Now she is the proud mommy of two beautiful little girls.

The Little Light House had helped literally thousands of children and their families over that period of time and the Little Light House scope of impact had reached a global scale.

The story of the development of the Little Light House was one of milestones and miracles, so much so I chronicled the whole amazing and God-authored story in my first book using those very words as the title, *Milestones & Miracles*.

As the elevator reached the second floor and the door slid open, I continued to reflect. I couldn't count the number of times over the years I had been asked the question: "Did you ever dream the Little Light House would become the internationally recognized model training center it is today?" Over and again, similar questions were posed to me. "Did you ever imagine that one day the Little Light House would be impacting children with special needs around the globe or that there would be a second Little Light House in another state?" My answer was always the same. It is humbling to even think about, and no, I never dreamed or imagined all that God would do in and through the ministry of the Little Light House. God knew better than to reveal His whole plan to me early on. I would never have had enough faith to move forward. But God, in His infinite wisdom, illuminated only one stepping stone at a time. Those stepping stones led to where we are today.

His power and grace have been dramatically manifested year after year, decade upon decade and undeniably, regardless of the size or scope of the ministry, He continues to show Himself faithful to this day.

Through the years, we have learned volumes. Many of the lessons we've learned have been through hard knocks and experiences, which can be a painful process. We're human, and we make mistakes, sometimes big ones. They may be mistakes made with the best of intentions, but mistakes nonetheless. We fall down and God, in His grace and mercy, gently helps us up, points us in the right direction, and gives us the courage to continue on.

Countless times, we've had to take a long, introspective look at these frailties and failures in the revealing light of God's Word. It has been in those times when God etched His Biblical principles on our hearts and along the way, these Biblical principles became the foundation and plumb line for everything the Little Light House does and stands for.

When the Board of Directors asked if I would document the Biblical principles so foundational to the Little Light House, I wondered where to even begin. Obviously, there was no way I could write about every Biblical principle contained in the Word of God. I knew I would need to narrow it down to the key principles which had become such a part of our DNA. This I have done.

These are just the primary principles. The rest you can find in His Holy Word! This is our story. These are some of the principles God has imparted to us.

They are, plain and simple, the primary operating principles our leadership has been committed to for years. I believe they are at the heart of how God has instructed us to do the work He has called us to do, the way He has called us to do it.

My prayer is that these pages have brought encouragement to the discouraged, faith to those who may have lost their way, understanding to those who are seeking, and courage and insights to those who would dare to respond to God's call on their life to do His work, His way.

Now to him who is able to do immeasurably
more than all we ask or imagine, according to his
power that is at work within us, to him be glory
in the church and in Christ Jesus throughout all
generations, for ever and ever! Amen.

– (Ephesians 3:20-21 NIV) –

For more information about the Little Light House:

Many of the documents referred to in *God's Work—God's Way* are available free of charge by contacting the Little Light House at 918-664-6746.

To learn more about the Little Light House or their International Training Program, call 918-664-6746 or visit their website at www.littlelighthouse.org.

The Little Light House curriculum, *Head to Toe, Heart and Soul,* is available free of charge through their online training center, www.thelittleanchor.org.

Author and founder of the Little Light House may be contacted through the Little Light House by calling 918-664-6746.

89296811R10100

Made in the USA
Columbia, SC
17 February 2018